TOPICS

1. SHAPES/SIZES
2. POOL BOTTOM DESIGN
3. FUNCTION Inlets/Skimmers
4. FUNCTION French Drain
5. FUNCTION Main Drain
6. FILTERS/HEATING/PUMPS
7. FUNCTION Filters/Pumps
8. FUNCTION Heaters
9. POOL TYPES
10. OPTIONAL EQUIPMENT Stairs
11. OPTIONAL EQUIPMENT Lights
12. DIVING BOARDS
13. SLIDES
14. SOLAR REELS
15. LADDERS/HANDRAILS
16. NEW CONSTRUCTION - Planning
17. NEW CONSTRUCTION - Design
18. NEW CONSTRUCTION - Layout
19. CONCRETE POOLS -Design & Plans
20. WHIRLPOOL/SPA - Plans
21. WHIRLPOOL/SPA - Filter/Heating
22. ADDITIONS/INDOOR POOLS
23. PONDS
24. PONDS - Function & Design
25. PONDS - Planning & Design
26. LINER POOLS
27. LINER POOLS - Plans
28. POOL WATER
29. CHEMICALS/MAINTENANCE TIPS
30. VACUUM/FILTER BACKWASH
31. FILTERING/PUMP LEAKS
32. SPRING POOL OPENINGS
33. WINTERIZING
34. WINTERIZING - Blowout Extensions
35. WINTERIZING - Cold & Ice Damage
36. WINTERIZING - Water & Cover Prep.
37. POOL EXCAVATING
38. POOL EXCAVATING - Liner/Concrete Pools
39. POOL EXCAVATING - Concrete
40. POOL PLUMBING
41. ELECTRICAL WORK
42. CONCRETE CONSTRUCTION
43. NEW POOL CONSTRUCTION
44. NEW CONSTRUCTION - Position
45. NEW CONSTRUCTION - Fences
46. NEW CONSTRUCTION - Lakeside Pools
47. FALL/WINTER CONSTRUCTION
48. MISC. CONSTRUCTION TIPS
49. REPAIRS - Filters/Pump/Heaters
50. REPAIRS - Plumbing
51. REPAIRS - Pools - All
52. REPAIRS - Liner Pool Rebuilding
53. DECKING - Finish & Expansion Joints
54. DECKING - Wire Mesh reinforcement
55. DECKING - Skimmers/Diving Board Jig
56. DECKING - Ladders & Handrails
57. GENERAL OVERVIEW
58. INTERESTING FACTS
59. PLANNING GUIDE
60. FOLIAGE ENHANCEMENTS
61. WORKSHEETS
62. SHAPES/SIZES TEMPLATE

SHAPES/SIZES

Inground pools are available in many shapes and sizes. The most popular shape is the true rectangle, available in 12 X 24, 14 X 26, 16 X 32, 18 X 36, and 20 X 40 ft.. The following radius corners can also be added : .5, 2, and 4.5 ft.. Hotel pools are usually rectangular with sharp 90 degree corners.

Residential pools always look more attractive with radius corners. Curvature provides the best water movement. It flows smoothly near curves, causing more water to be skimmed, filtered, and treated.

A swimming pool must be planned and designed to mix heat and chemicals evenly with the total water supply. Many inlets are used: (H-2-O returns), a bottom hopper main drain (H-2-O intake), two skimming units (H-2-O intakes) and a powerful filter/pump system.

To illustrate the difficulty of successfully achieving the above mixture, imagine a bathtub full of cool water. Hot water and bath soap (ie: pool chemicals) are introduced at the tap. The hot water/soap must be mixed to arrive at a new higher temperature/bath soap concentration. (Concentration is often expressed in parts per million)

The difficulty of mixing hot water and soap in the tub is multiplied immeasurably when mixing 18,000 gallons of water with heat and chemicals in a swimming pool 16 ft. wide by 32 ft. long. It is not an easy task.

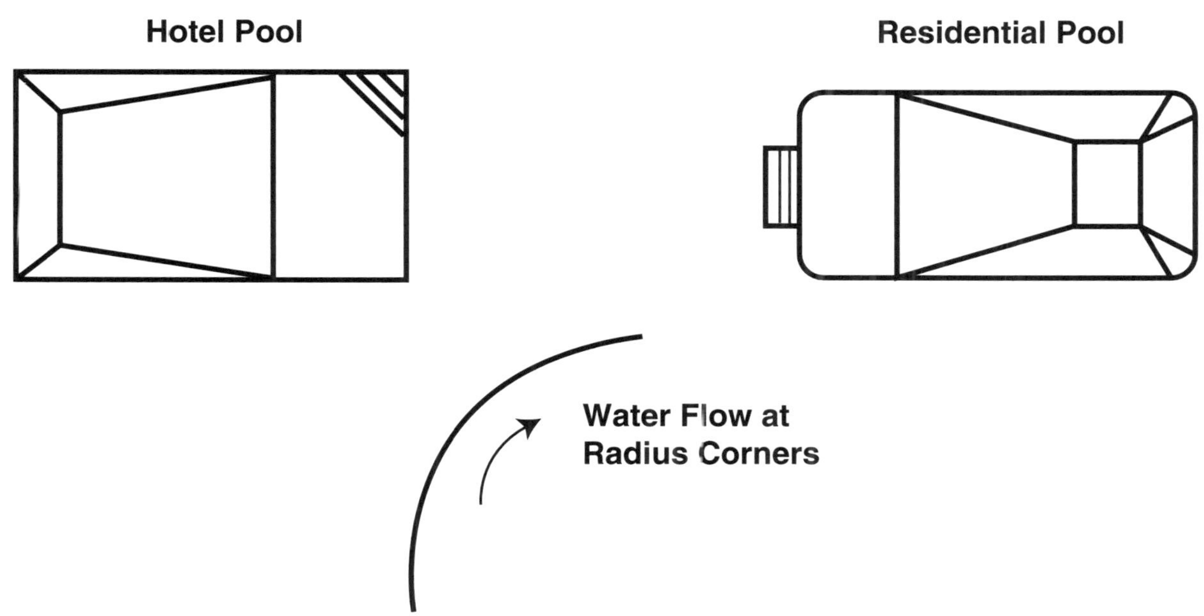

SHAPES/SIZES

When choosing a pool shape and size consider the 16 X 32 ft. rectangle with 2 ft. radius corners. It's a perfect size pool for everyone. It is economical, and large enough for diving, swimming laps, volleyball, etc.. The shallow end is (8.5 X 16 ft.) and the remaining area (23.5 X 16 ft.) (deep end) is large enough for serious swimming fun.

Inground pools are designed with a very large deep area. This is because more square footage is favorable and is needed for proper installation. Diving, swimming, and underwater activities require a slight abyss. The incline is at a slight taper: (19.0 degrees), and the back walls/sidewalls are pitched: (49.0 degrees).

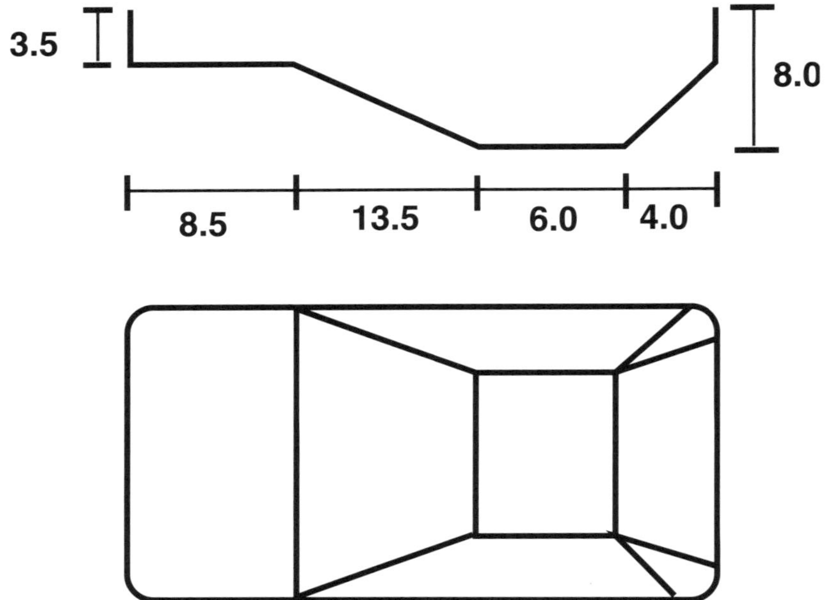

The water capacity is 18,000 gallons, actually less than most inground pools. The 16 x 32 ft. pool is more economical to heat, and will save you money on chemicals, electric and repairs.

Larger pools have a 30,000 (plus) gallon water capacity. You will spend 40% more on chemicals, heat and electric. The 16 x 32 ft. pool is the industry standard size: thus, cost for accessories and parts is less. Seriously consider the 16 x 32 for recreation, size, economy, and improved function.

Another popular shape is the Grecian. Designed for backyards with limited room, this pool can fit into tight spots. Angled corners offer a unique, yet attractive style. Available in many sizes: 14 x 28, 16 x 32, 20 x 32, and 20 x 40 ft.. The 20 ft. width is very nice looking, adding luxury to your backyard. The Grecian is a contemporary design.

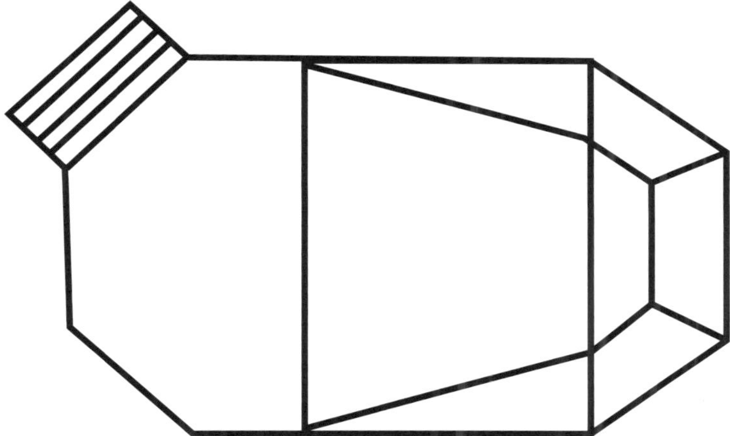

Free form pools can be any shape or size. Usually constructed with large, flowing radius corners, the free form will enhance and beautify your backyard.

Choose from Kidney, Mountain Lake, Figure Eight or self design shapes. The Kidney is the most popular, with: 16 x 30, 16 x 34, and 20 x 38 ft..

The cost is usually prohibitive. Free-forming pools are expensive to build, repair and buy accessories for.

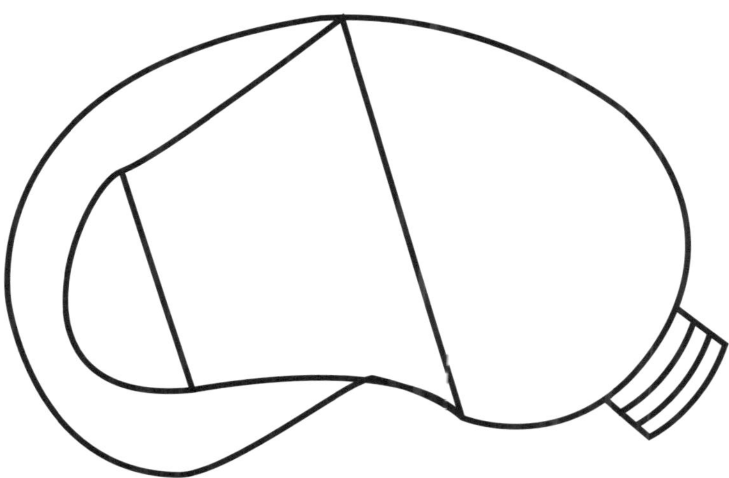

SHAPES/SIZES

If you would like a larger pool, consider the L-series. There are two types: True L and Lazy L. Available in many sizes ranging from 16 x 38 x 24 ft. to 19 x 45 ft.. The L-shaped pools are for larger backyards.

The shallow area is very large, and will add that extra needed room for playing games, lounging, etc..

And now add radius corners:

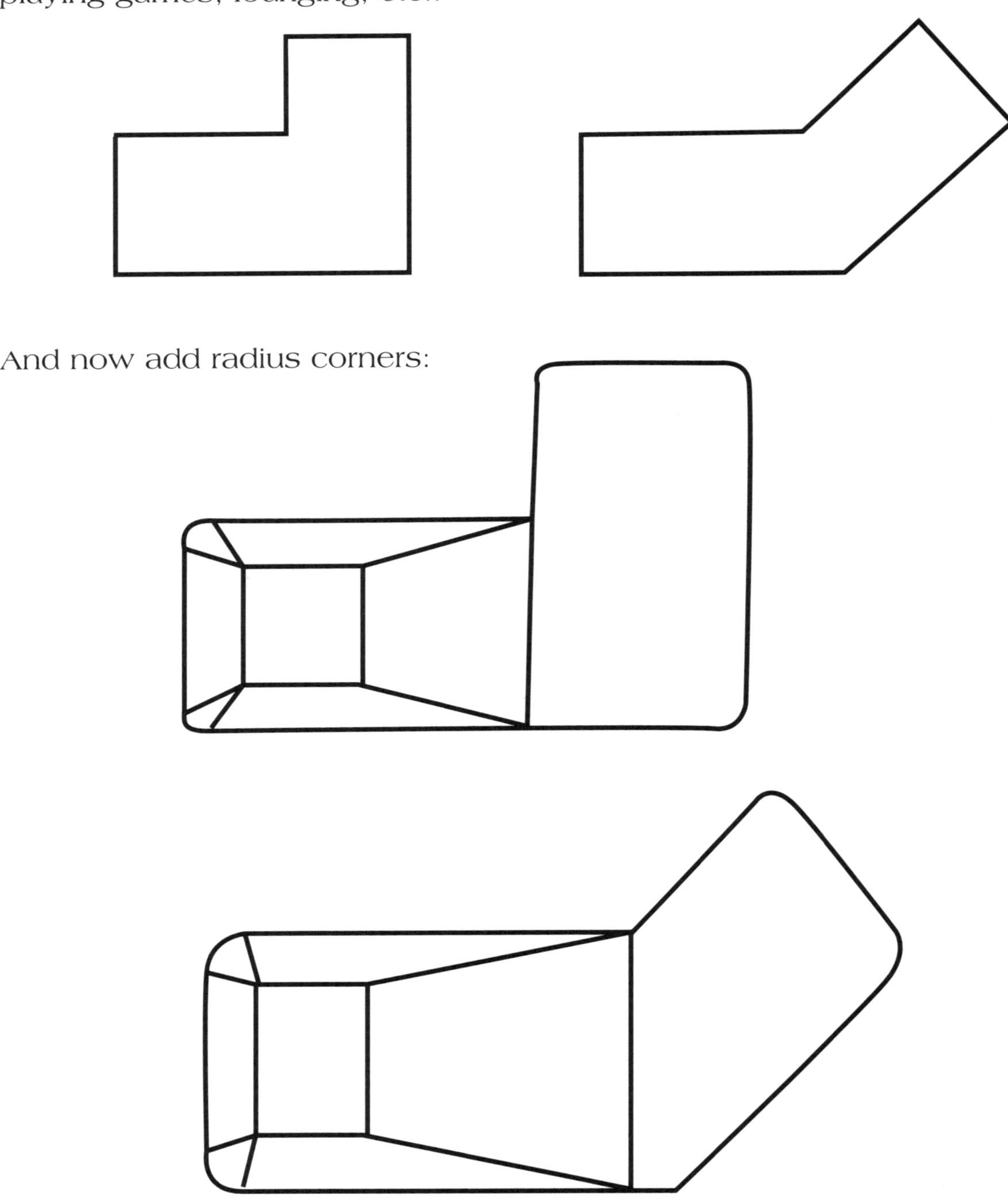

The Patio Pool is a compact pool that features plenty of swimming area. Complete with shallow and deep ends, it is available in two sizes: 21 x 21 ft. and 26 x 26 ft.. The Patio Pool can be positioned in very tight areas. An attractive octagonal shape, the Patio Pool becomes an extension of your existing patio.

This pool is inexpensive to build, heat and maintain.

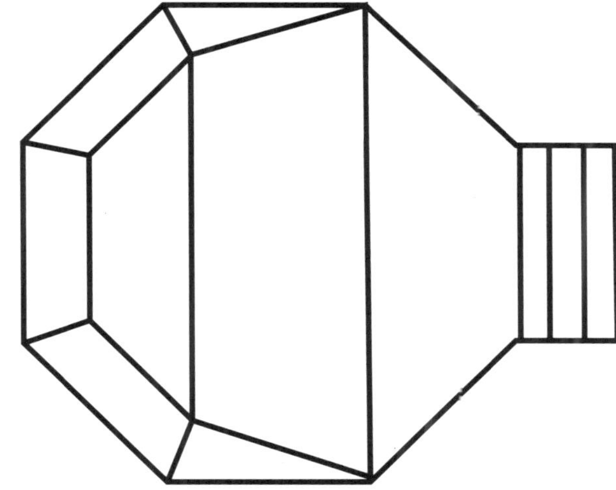

There are a few other shapes you can choose from.

1. **Oval**
2. **Roman End**
3. **Rectangle with diagonal corners**
4. **Grecian Lazy L**

The Oval is a nice looking design that features a large radius on each end. Built for beauty and function, the true oval is a pool that others resem-ble.

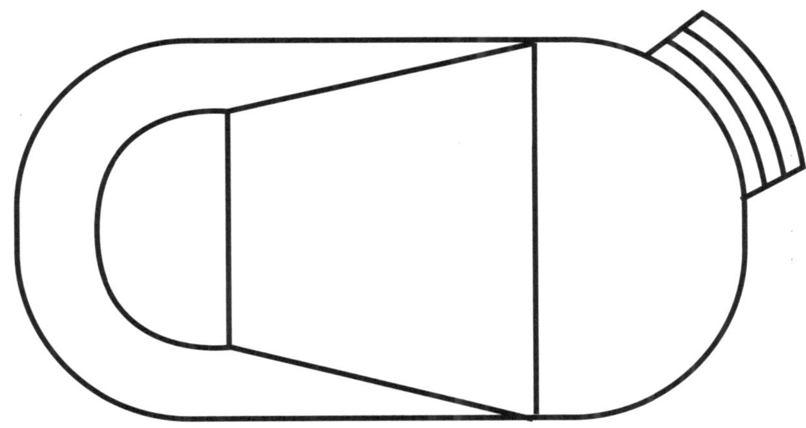

Roman End Pools

Roman End Pools resemble early Roman design. Large radius ends with two smaller radius coves make the Roman End Pool both unique and stylish. Although it is not a very popular design, it has some very nice features.

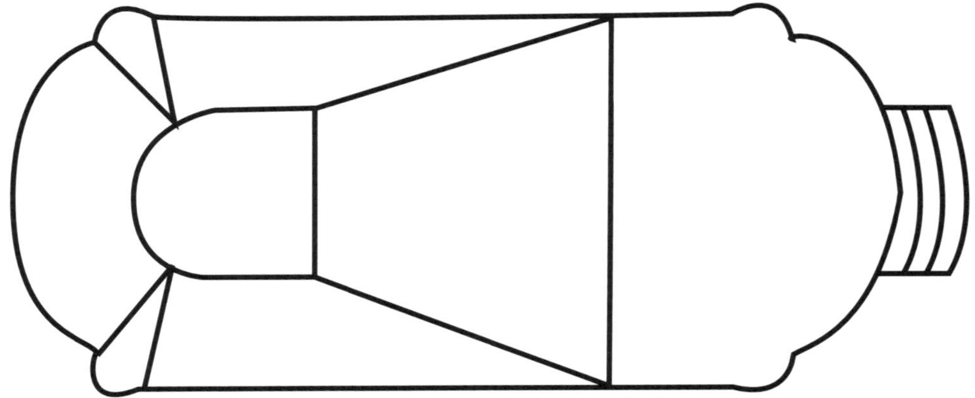

Rectangle shape with diagonal corners

The basic Rectangle with diagonal corners is one of the earliest designs. The more contemporary designs don't use diagonal much any more, but they are still available.

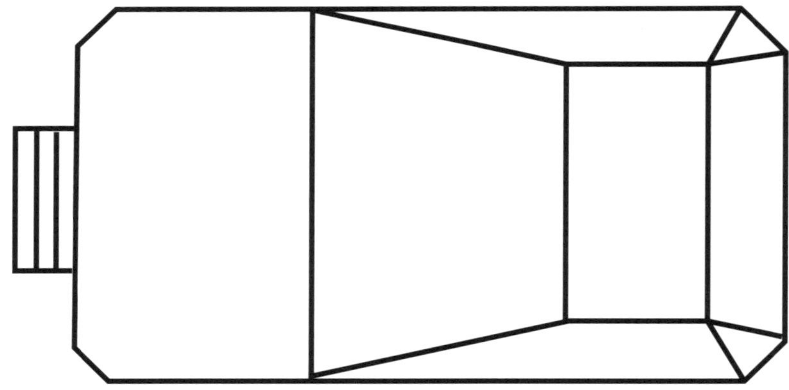

Grecian Lazy L Pools

The Grecian Lazy L is a combination of the Grecian and the L series. Designed for large backyards, the Grecian Lazy L features a large swimming area and unique design.

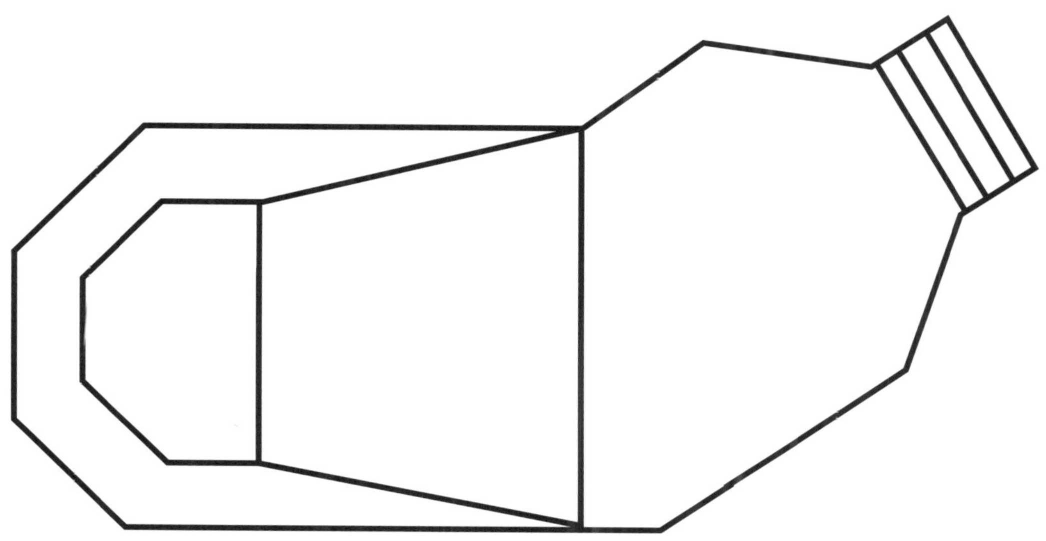

POOL BOTTOM DESIGN

Most pools are classified: **Diving and Non-diving**. Diving pools range from 3-8 ft. deep, and include a shallow end, incline, hopper and back/side walls. Standard pool specifications are designed by the National Swimming Pool Institute (NSPI). The Institute has developed specifications for all inground swimming pools. These specifications are adopted to promote safety, and improve swimming pool construction.

The standard diving pool has a 8.5 ft. shallow end, 13.5 ft. incline, 6.0 ft. hopper and 4.0 ft. back/side walls. The incline slope is roughly 19 degrees, a slight taper for improved diving.

A 8 ft. deep end promotes safety and swimmability. The deep area provides plenty of room for swimming and diving. Pool specifications can be altered for different applications.

Non-diving pools range from 3-6 ft. deep and also include a shallow end, incline, hopper and back/side walls. Smaller pools are usually non-diving; size/shape: 12 x 24, 14 X 26/rectangle, 21 X 21/patio pool. There simply isn't enough room in the deep area for the proper incline pitch. Larger pool plans can be changed to non-diving. Depths can range from 4.5-7.0 ft..

A sport pool is a non-diving bottom design, converting the pool into a functional, fun area. Equipped with a center volleyball net, basketball area and slide, this design features two shallow ends, two inclines and a hopper strip 1-3 ft. wide.

Sport pools have been around for about 7 years and are installed frequently. The cost is slightly higher because of the non-standard design. A sport bottom usually has more square footage and the depth ranges from 4.5-6.5 ft.. Shallow ends, inclines, and hopper strips are adjusted accordingly.

The sport pool has some advantages over conventional pools. The significant decrease in water capacity will allow you to save 20-30% on chemicals and heating. This provides a warmer, more economical pool system.

The installation of additional water inlets can provide a swim-whirlpool effect because of increased water temperature and improved heating efficiency.

POOL BOTTOM DESIGN

The standard diving pool is widely preferred and frequently installed. Many people enjoy the large deep area for diving, underwater activities, etc.. Diving is sometimes limited to a non-spring board, decreasing the amount of horseplay and homeowner liability. An eight ft. deep end is both safe and practical for swimming fun. Below is the basic pool bottom design for all inground swimming pools.

POOL BOTTOM IDENTIFICATION

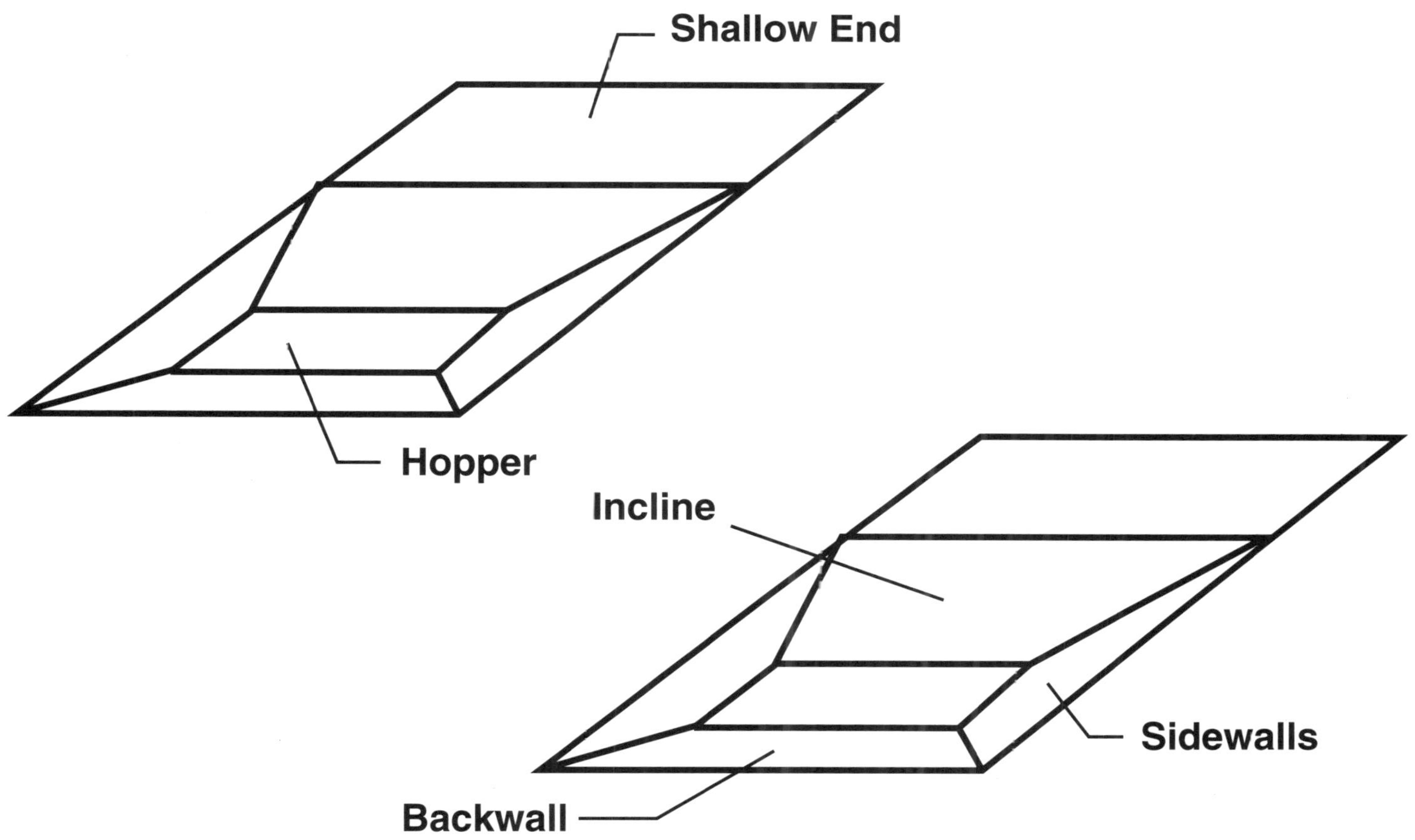

Inground pools must be carefully planned, designed and installed. There are two things to consider:

1. **Pool structure and longevity**
2. **Pool water function**

Lets take a look at function. The pool should function at the lowest cost and maximum performance. This is accomplished by using a overrated pump (1.5 HP) and a large enough sand tank (250-300 lb.). We install a automatic 24 hr. timer to operate the filter system between midnight and 6:00 AM. The electric rates are lower at these times. We are trying to completely turn over the total water capacity. Most pumps run at 80-100 gallons per minute. The 1.5 HP pump will operate at 120 gpm, providing more suction at the skimmers, maindrain and more water flow at the inlets.

Inlets should be positioned opposite skimmers: two at the shallow, two in the deep area, one in the center, and two installed at the stairs to clean and provide a whirlpool effect. Inlets are set at a 37 degree angle to the pool surface for maximum water velocity. Your center inlet can be hooked into a slide to provide warm, chlorinated water on the slide surface.

Two skimmers should be positioned on the house side and closest to your patio to aid in skimmer maintenance. Skimmers remove the water from the top surface in an effort to remove debris.

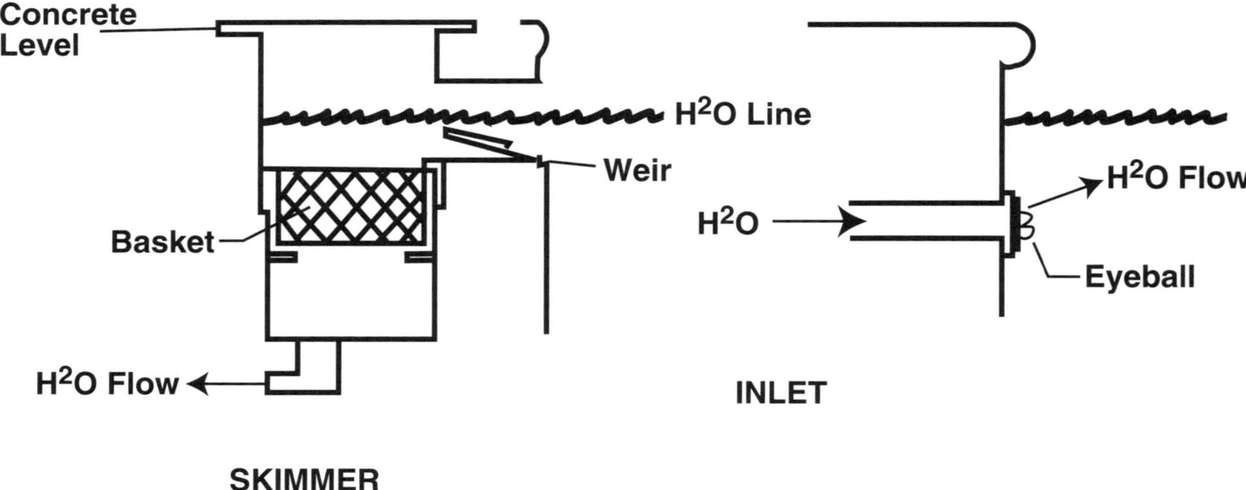

Skimmer baskets trap leaves, silt, bugs and debris from the surface. Water velocity is increased with use of a skimmer weir. The weir is drawn downward from the suction of the pump. The automatic skimmers serve to clean and circulate the water supply. Some auto-cleaners plug into the skimmer. The vacuum suction plate is placed above the skimmer basket while vacuuming. The skimmer is an important part of pool function.

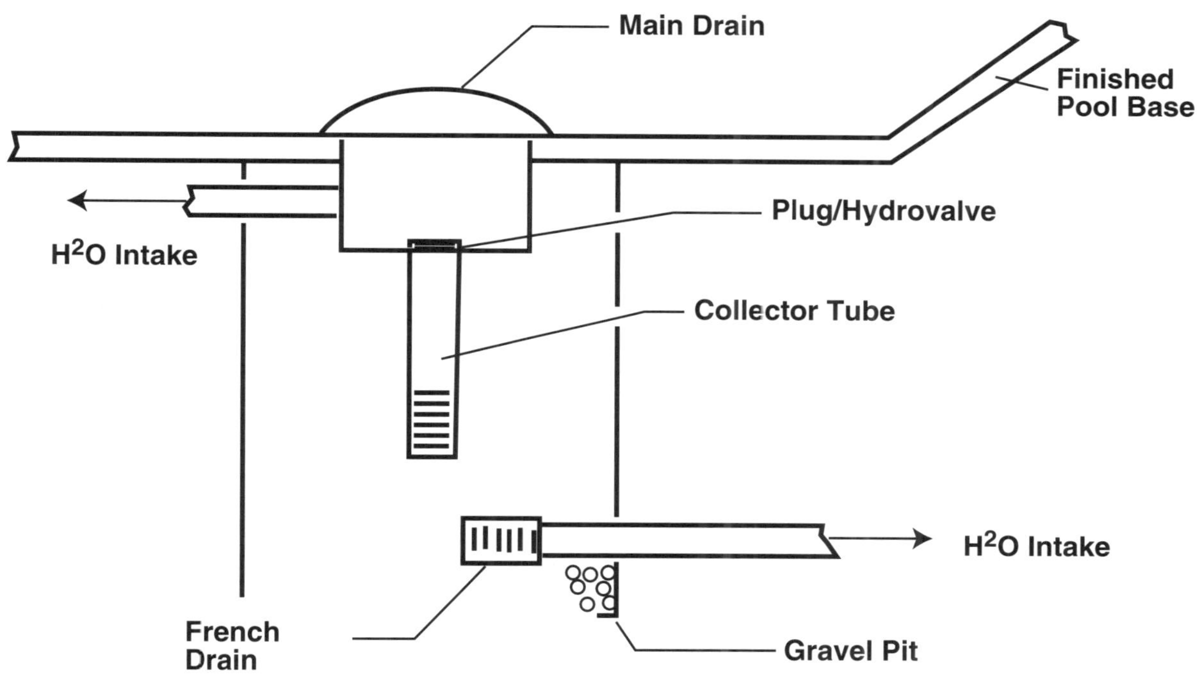

The maindrain is located at the bottom center of the deep end. This is a water intake. The drain enables the colder, untreated water on the bottom to be filtered, heated and chlorinated. It can also be used to lower the pool water level. It serves as another functional component to maximize performance of the pool water treating system.

Note:

In a gravel pit below the main drain, a foot valve (french drain) is installed. This is a valve which draws ground water from under the main drain to keep the pool work area clean and dry during pool construction. The french drain is a vital component to ongoing pool operation. Connect the french drain to the filter/pump system to draw ground water from under the pool to increase the water capacity, providing an extra water supply. (However there must be ground water at a 10ft depth).

Schematic of H^2O Flow

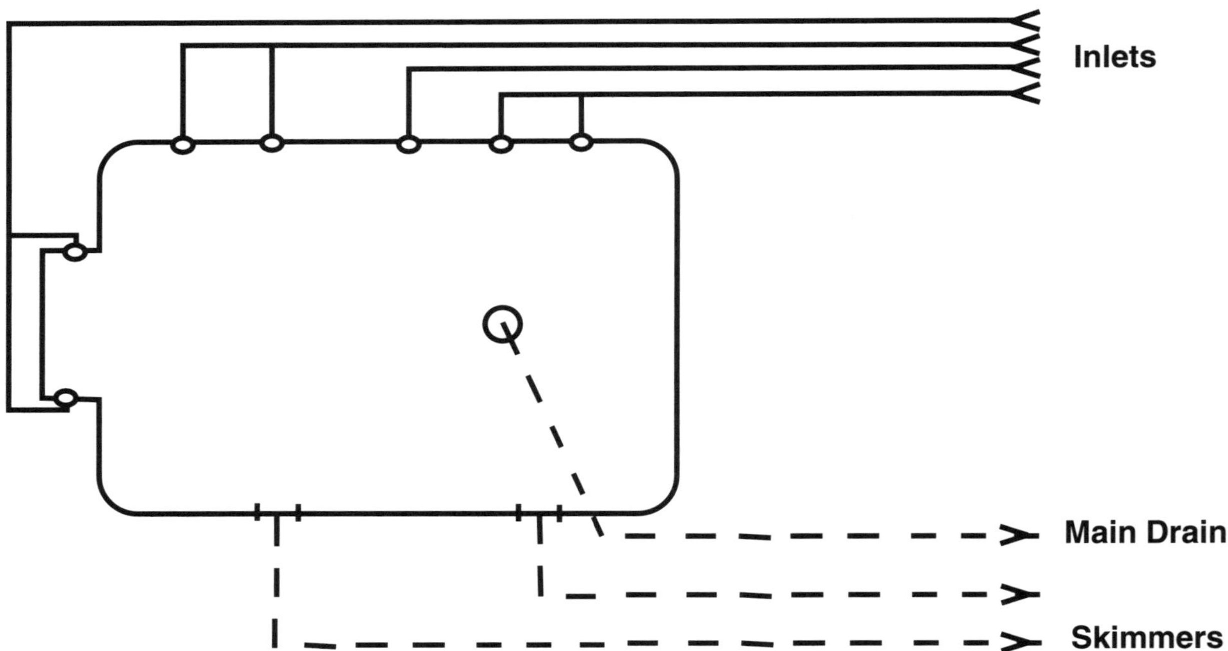

Most inground pools are equipped with a filtering system. One type is a sand filter. Sand is the medium (filter material) used to trap bacteria and particles. The water is pushed by the pump and into the filter tank. There the water is drawn through the sand. Sand filters are common, featuring less maintenance and easy operation. Atop the filter is a multi-port valve system, that allows you to choose filtering positions: **BACKWASH, RINSE, FILTER, RECIRCULATE, and CLOSE.** Upon normal operation, the valve is in the **FILTER** position. After many smaller particles are trapped in the sand, the pressure gauge will read 20-30 psi (Normal filtering pressure is 10-16 psi). At this point you must **BACKWASH** your filtering system. Select **BACKWASH** position on the multi-port valve and view the site glass. When the water is clear turn the pump off. Select **RINSE**. Turn pump on and view the siteglass. Then select **FILTER** (normal position). You must backwash once a week and after vacuuming.

BACKWASHING SUMMARY:

PUMP	MULTI-PORT POSITION	EXPLANATION
off		
on	Backwash	to clean sand
off		
on	Rinse	to clean sand
off		
on	Filter	normal operation

Most sand filters are 20-30 inches in diameter. Sand capacity is 200-300 lbs. Silica sand should range from .450 to .55mm diameter. After a period of time, the diameter size will decrease due to friction between the water and sand. Upon decreasing diameter the filter/pump will back-up slightly, and sand may flow from the inlets. Be sure to change filter sand every year to ensure maximum performance of the filter/pump system. Select a filter tank that splits in half to assist in easy sand removal/installation.

Cartridge filter elements are used when certain municipalities prohibit backwashing into city sewer systems. The water is circulated through a paper type filter, and backwashing is not required; however, you must remove and clean the cartridge periodically. Earth filters are frequently used with above ground pools. Filter tanks contain disks, which are coated with diatomaceous earth. This is called charging. Earth is very messy and backwashing is required. Earth filters trap particles 1/10 the size of any other type of filter.

FILTER SUMMARY:

	BACKWASHING	MAINTENANCE	FILTERING
Sand	yes	least	best
Cartridge	no	most	least
Earth	yes	most	best

The pool pump is the heart of a functional water flow system. Choose a 1.0-1.5 HP overrated, more expensive pump ($350-$450). The trick is to overrate, to promote less water turn-over time. Overrating provides a longer pump life. The pump must run 5-8 hrs. a day, usually after 12 midnight, to completely filter your total water supply. There is a basket inside your pump which has to be cleaned periodically.

Pump motors arrive from the factory 115 or 220 voltage hook-up. Choose the 115 voltage to extend the life of electrical parts inside the motor.

Pumps should be hooked into a 24 hr timer to provide the exact start/finish times; thus, preventing under/over filtering. Make sure water is always flowing into the lint pot, by visual inspection.

CONVENTIONAL PUMP

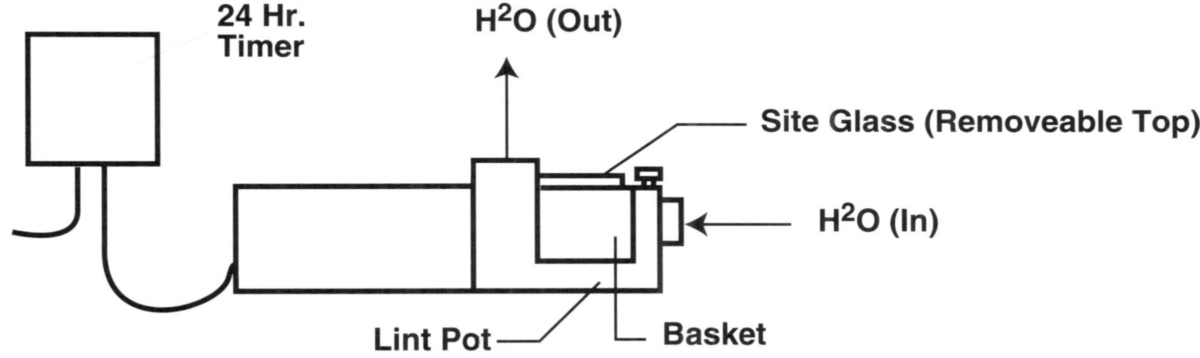

There are several types of pool heaters: Natural gas, Electric, and Solar. Natural gas is the most popular because it cost less to operate. Natural gas and electric heaters are free standing (vertical). Some natural gas features are:

Copper pipe heat exchanger unit
Cast iron water headers complete with dual water hook-ups
Burner tray complete with orifices
Gas valve
Pressure switch

There are two hook-ups, gas and water. First consider the gas line and valve. The gas is introduced into the gas valve, where the pilot assembly (thermocoupler) draws gas for pilot lighting. When the heater is switched on, the main burner tray is lit, providing extreme heat to the copper exchanger, where the pool water is heated. A rheostat controls pool water temperature. The amount of heat used is expressed in BTU's. Natural gas heaters are available in many sizes: 60,000, 125,000, 150,000, 200,000, 250,000, 325,000. The rating is based on top surface square footage:

16 X 32	**500 sq. ft.**	**125,000 BTU heater**
18 X 36	**640 sq. ft.**	**200,000 BTU heater**
20 X 40	**800 sq. ft.**	**250,000 BTU heater**

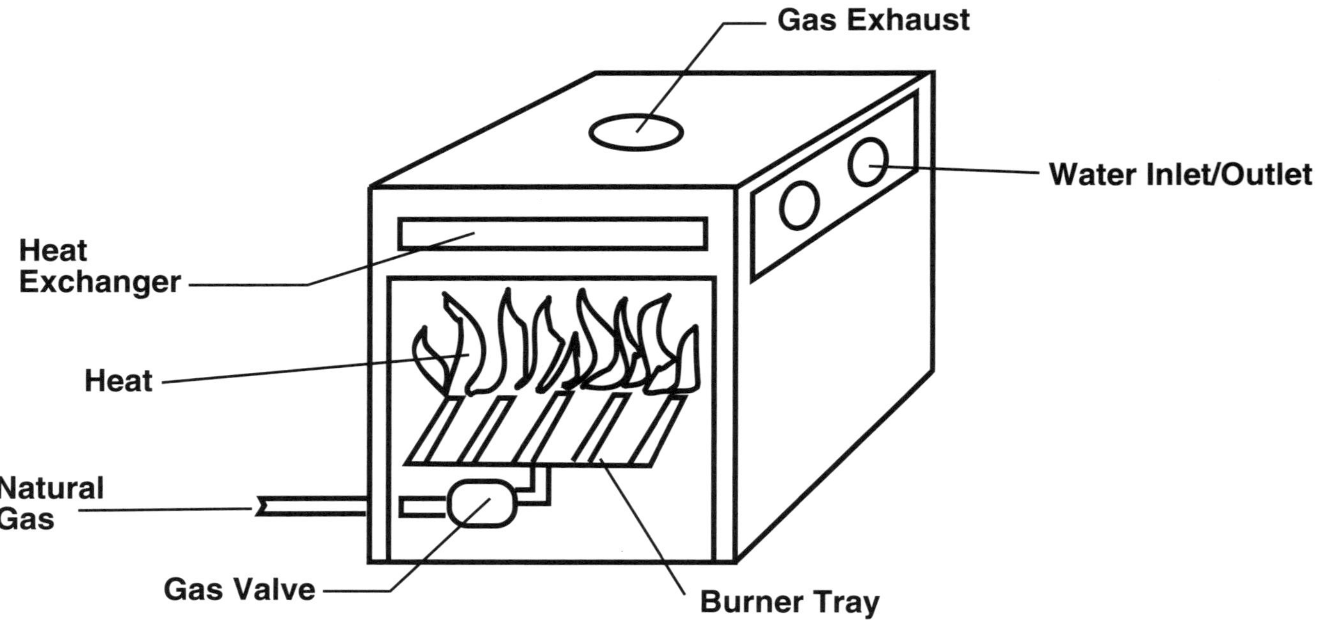

The real trick to pool heating is to heat the pool only once a week, for example, Friday, raising the pool temperature from 77 degrees to 82 degrees. Then install the solar cover to prevent water evaporation and heat loss. Use the pool all weekend long. During the week leave the heater completely off. This will save 70% on the gas bill. A constant water temperature does not have to be maintained. Make sure to buy the more expensive, overrated heater to save time and money.

Electric heaters are very expensive to operate. 1.5-5.0 KW are available. These heaters convert electrical energy into heat. Most spas use an in-line electric heater that is somewhat slow.

Solar heaters work very well; in fact using a solar heater in conjunction with a gas heater will save substantially on the gas bill; however, solar panels are very expensive. A conventional system can cost from $2-8,000 dollars. An alternate solution is to construct your own solar system. I have designed a conventional solar system with a cost as low as $350.
Here is the plan.

SOLAR HEATER

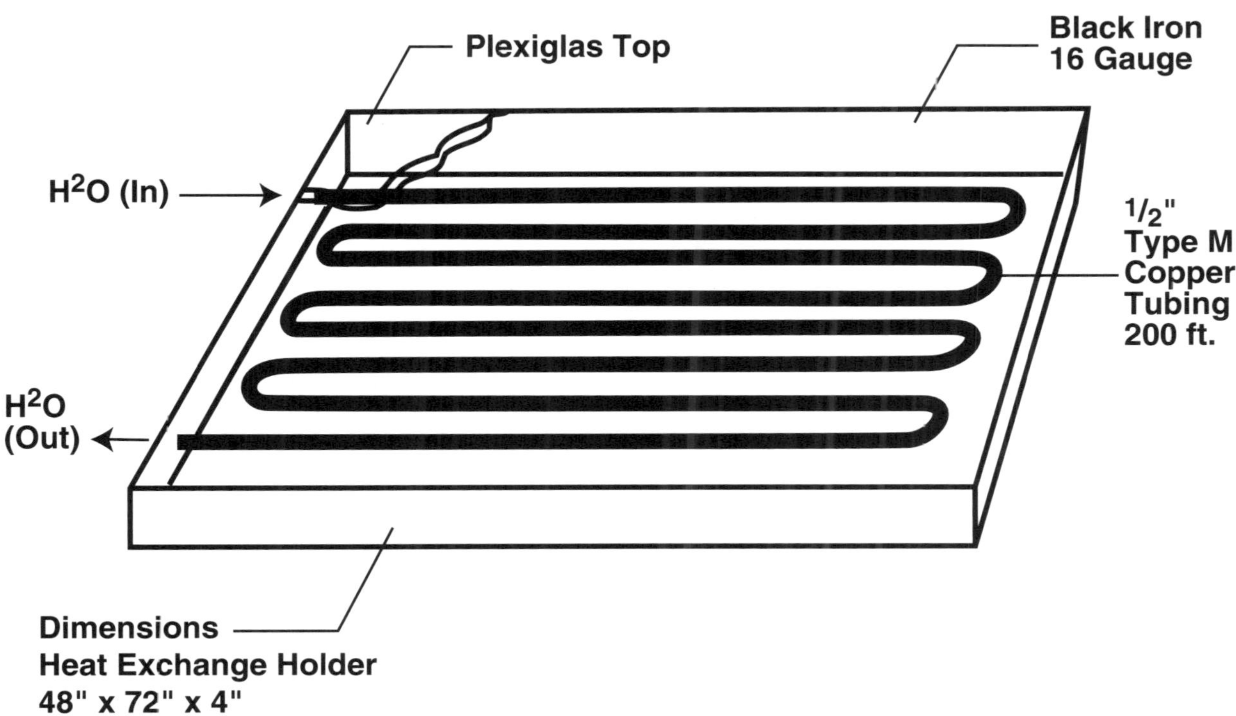

POOL TYPES

There are several types of inground pools, we will discuss five different styles:

1. **Steel wall/vinyl liner**
2. **Poured concrete walls/bottom**
3. **Fiberglass backed acrylic walls/concrete bottom**
4. **Gunite/Marcite**
5. **One Piece Fiberglass shell**

The steel wall/liner pool is the most economical, as well as the lowest maintenance. Algae, dirt and debris slide right off the vinyl and are easily removed. Inground liners do not stain very easily; in fact, there is an anti-bacterial film that is applied at the factory. Liners adhere to walls and sides with water pressure. The newest liners are designed and manufactured to last for many years; especially in northern winter conditions. Liner pools hold up better than any other pool to adverse conditions. The wall panels are 14 gauge steel (just under 1/8 inch thickness) coated with a zinc plating, (2.75 oz. per sq. inch) rated G-235. They are designed to last for years without rusting and warranted for up to 40 years. Steel is very strong and ductile, very well suited for the extreme weight and pressures associated with an inground pool, and well designed for extreme weather conditions. The steel wall/liner pool is the most popular pool in the northern climates and widely liked in the south as well.

The steel wall is locked into an outside concrete footing 6-12 inches thick. The wall and footing act as one. This structure is so strong a small home can be built on top of this wall. Most builders use rebar to lock this wall into place along with the concrete footing. A G-235 rated steel wall will last for years.

The pool base is vermiculite/cement mixture, light weight, strong, and self-supporting. Wall foam is then applied to the walls, adding insulation and liner protection. The concrete finish edge is a sandstone finish: white solid aluminum. The liner pool is a design that will last for years with the least maintenance.

POURED CONCRETE WALLS/BOTTOM

The poured concrete walls/bottom is best indoors or for warmer climates. Concrete pools feature real tile border, white marcite bottoms and attractive included whirlpool.

Concrete pools are somewhat more difficult to clean and maintain. Staining is a common problem. Water balance is especially important and care must be taken to maintain a PH level of 7.5.
The concrete pool can be a step above if properly installed and maintained. Many concrete pools are installed outside in the northern climates. Many apartment complexes use concrete as a gunite substitute to save large sums of money. Gunite is a lightweight, strong type of concrete aggregate. Concrete pools should last for 10 years plus without any repairs.
Concrete pools are a generic gunite pool with a stair included the width of the pool. Marcite offers a flowing pool interior with a slightly rough surface that adds a certain decorative style.

A poured concrete pool is a good solid structure. Many hotel and apartment complexes use concrete pools to save money. Concrete pools, plans, and construction methods are discussed in the concrete pool section. These pools feature real tile, a white marcite bottom and a decorative cap. Concrete pools can be installed outdoors or can be enclosed (see section on additions). At any rate, the concrete pool will hold-up to adverse conditions if installed properly.

GUNITE/MARCITE:

The cornerstone of all inground swimming pools, the Gunite pool is superior in design and beauty. Rows of small tile are located at the waterline and can be located on the stairs and on the enclosed whirlpools. Beauty, sophistication and flowing bottom contour are common with the Gunite pool. Most hotel pools are Gunite design, a very expensive concrete that is applied with air over rebar. Marcite is then applied to the bottom and sides.
Gunite pools are frequently installed outdoors in the south and southwest. There are many gunite pools in the north as well.

FIBERGLASS BACKED ACRYLIC WALLS/CONCRETE BOTTOM

Fiberglass backed acrylic walls/concrete bottom is a design used for many years. Acrylic is very attractive and durable. The walls are made for residential (42" wall) and for commercial (48" wall). Angle iron is used to reinforce the walls, and a concrete footing is poured. The walls are sealed with a bead of silicone. Neoprene is used at the wall joints. Most builders paint the concrete bottom. Repainting is necessary after 6 years. Newly manufactured acrylic is extremely resilient and will withstand sunlight, chemicals, and extreme temperature changes. White paint is usually used on the bottom and staining can occur. Smaller tile can actually be installed on the entire bottom.

Marcite can be applied to the bottom as well. These pools feature non maintenance attractive acrylic. Many hotel/apartment pools are acrylic.

ONE PIECE FIBERGLASS SHELL

A one piece molded shell design is best for indoor applications. Fiberglass is attractive, comfortable, inexpensive and will last for years. Most of these pools are smaller because of the one piece design. They feature a shallow end, incline and deep area. Normally the depth is 6 ft.. The shell is available in many colors; white, blue, etc.. The structure is very similar to a whirlpool and must be carefully installed.

Many fiberglass pools are installed outdoors. This can be an interesting challenge to many homeowners. They can be easily cleaned by emptying and refilling. Fiberglass pools are rarely considered for residential outdoor installation. Most homeowners buy liner, concrete or gunite pools.

Stairs OPTIONAL EQUIPMENT

Stairs are very popular because they add beauty and are very functional. With jets installed the stairs act as a whirlpool. Stairs are white fiberglass, reinforced with a space age material called Rovel. There are several styles available.

Stairs are available in 4, 6 and 8 ft. lengths. 8 ft. is the most common length. You can choose from 3-tread, 4-tread, or a step-n'- lounge.

Easy entrance/exit is a major advantage. Inlets can be installed to keep the stairs clean and act as an independent whirlpool system.

The walk-in stairs are an extension and a complement to your inground swimming pool. Moderately priced, stairs must be seriously considered when building an inground swimming pool.

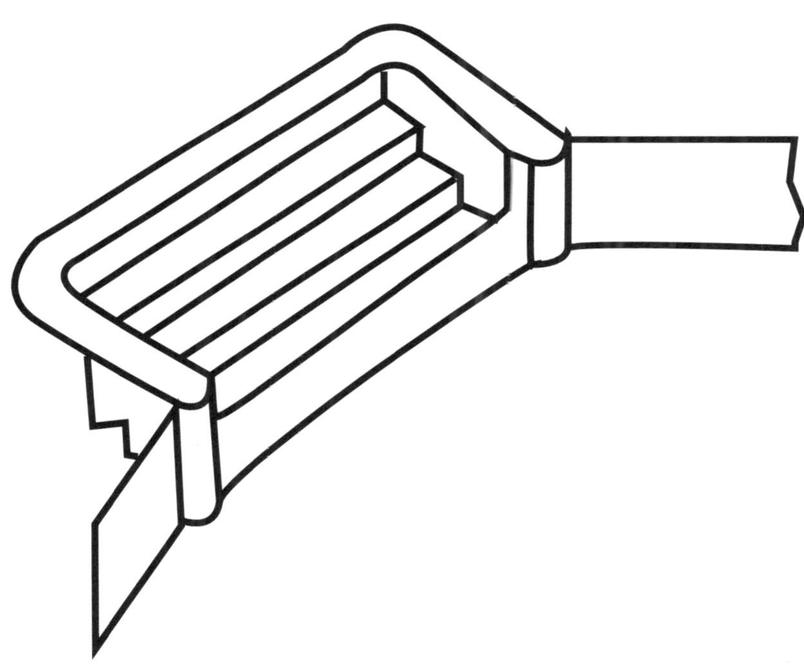

OPTIONAL EQUIPMENT Lights

There are two types of inground pool lights:

1. **Wet niche**
2. **Dry niche**

The wet niche is approved by the National Electric Code. A niche is a stainless steel container that is installed behind your swimming pool wall. The niche actually holds water and is the housing for the light assembly. Connected to the niche is a light conduit, usually plastic, which is connected to a junction box.

The light assembly consists of a light bulb, lens, and a waterproof sealing unit. Two lights are available:

1. 300 watt/12 volt
2. 400 watt/ 115 volt

The 300 watt/12 volt is preferred. A 12 volt transformer is connected in-line to reduce the voltage to 12 volts, which is safer, and will extend the bulb life. The pool light, positioned at the deep end center, will provide plenty of water lighting. To remove the light assembly, simply unscrew the top mounting screw, and move assembly to pool decking. To remove bulb, unscrew waterproof light assembly and replace bulb. To reinstall assembly lock bottom tab and screw in top mounting screw.

Pool lights are popular and widely used. They enhance and complement the surrounding pool area. Colored lenses can be added and are easily attached. A light must be carefully considered before the pool installation because one cannot be installed afterward.

A dry niche is available, although not approved in many areas. The installation is minimal and is merely a three inch hole. Dry niches are fairly new, featuring a low-water cut-off, futuristic design and improved maintenance. Halogen bulbs replace conventional lighting. The real advantage is extended assembly life. Dry niches eliminate water in the niche and in the light conduit, providing a trouble-free lighting system.

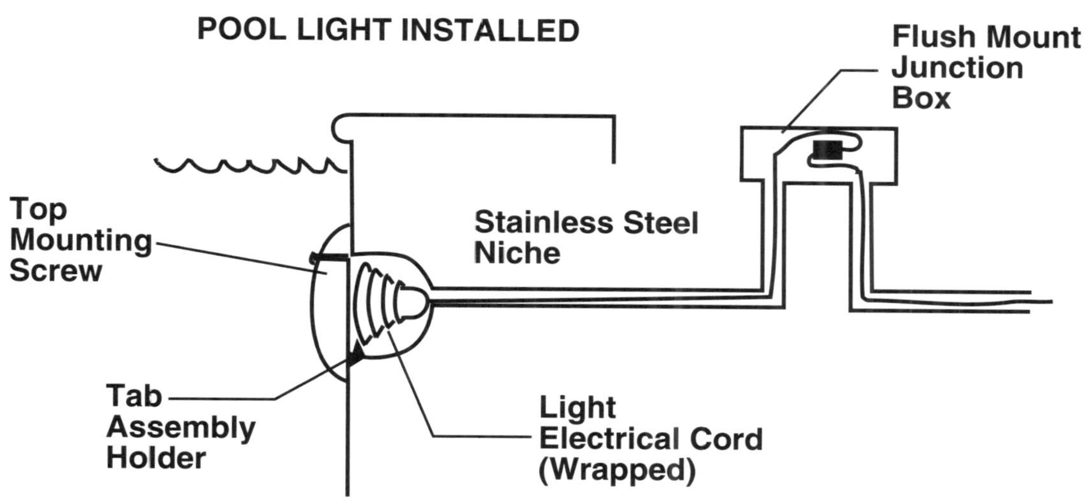
POOL LIGHT INSTALLED
Flush Mount Junction Box
Top Mounting Screw
Stainless Steel Niche
Tab Assembly Holder
Light Electrical Cord (Wrapped)

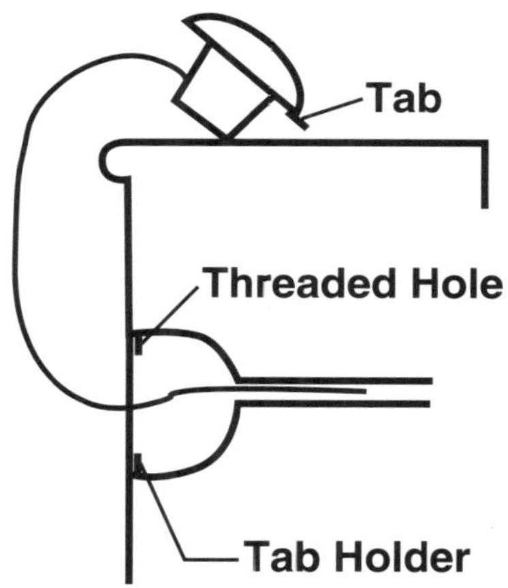
REMOVAL/INSTALLATION OF LIGHT ASSEMBLY
Tab
Threaded Hole
Tab Holder

DIVING BOARDS

There are two types of boards:

1. **Non-spring**
2. **Spring**

Non-spring boards are the most popular and widely used. They decrease liability and limit the amount of horseplay. These boards are also nice looking. Two sizes should be considered for residential; 6 and 8 ft..

The base is called the diving stand and is complete with fulcrum and board attachment. Made of fiberglass reinforced acrylic, the stand is both strong and attractive, with a white textured finish.

The board is usually constructed with a wood core, and sealed to a acrylic surface. A white board with the white base is a non-oxidizing, long lasting combination.

A diving board jig is usually installed before the pool concrete decking is poured. The jig connects to the diving stand.

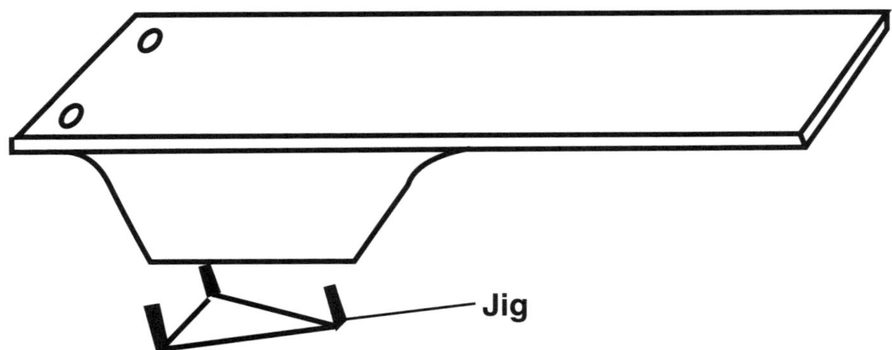

Slides are really fun and exciting to use. The 8 ft. Queen shoots you right off the slide end.

An aluminum ladder is attached to the fiberglass molded slide body. The slide must be properly installed to insure sturdiness and functionality.

The water supplying the slide jets should be the pool water. A center inlet should be installed so a line can be connected from the center inlet to the slide water lines. Purchase a white slide to avoid any fading from chlorine oxidation.

Slides should be positioned opposite the house side. A right or left curve is available. They add a new dimension to your swimming area.

The slide mounts to the concrete with plastic flanges supplied from the slide manufacturer. Set the slide lag bolts into the concrete as the concrete is being poured. A better method is to install the slide after the concrete is poured. Position the slide in the desired location, then drill into the concrete and use concrete anchoring bolts. I have designed a special stainless steel plate that will secure the slide ladder to the concrete, providing more support;

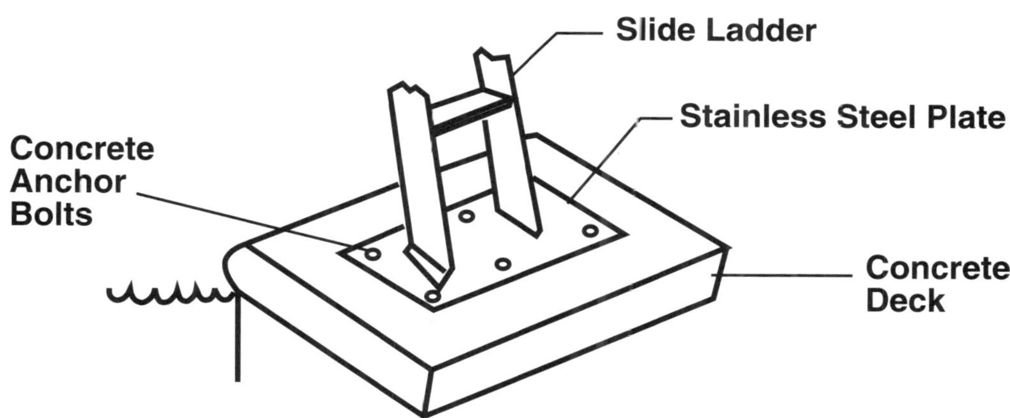

SOLAR REELS

Solar reels have increased in popularity. They feature a manual hand reeling system to remove/attach the solar cover.

There is an automatic reel system complete with a remote controller; however, the cost is prohibitive.

Choose an inground quality extruded aluminum rolling shaft with a low profile. Solar reels are an important convenience because solar covers are difficult to remove and install. Solar covers should be on the pool surface when the pool is not in use to decrease heat loss and chemical dissipation. Also a solar cover will help keep leaves and debris out of the pool.

Installing the solar reel system from the factory is troublesome, so be sure to enlist plenty of help.

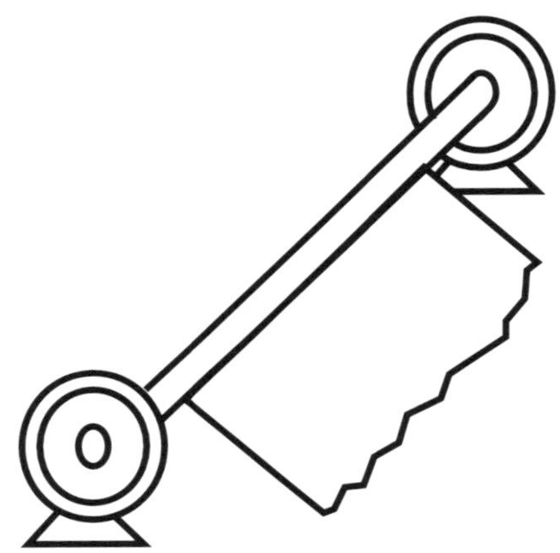

LADDERS/HANDRAILS

Ladders/Handrails should be stainless steel and 1.90 inches in diameter. There are two types of ladders:

1. Coping
2. Concrete

The coping ladder mounts to the pool wall and the anchors are submersed in concrete. Coping ladders are curved inward towards the pool. The coping ladder is available in three tread plastic stairs.

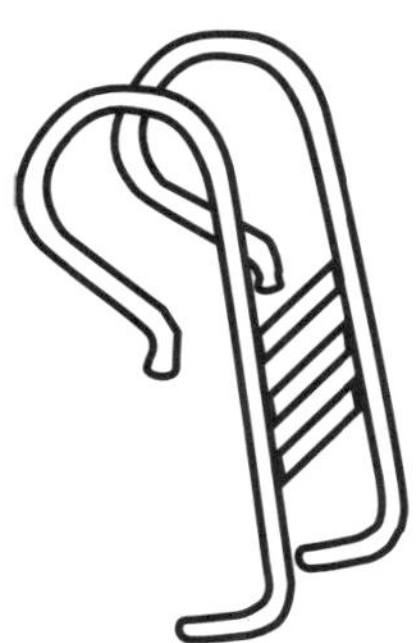

The conventional concrete ladder mounts into a metal extension and the anchors are set in concrete. The ladder is removable for winterizing, cleaning and maintenance. A 3-4 inch brass anchor is used to mount the ladder into pool decking. Ladders are positioned 10-15 ft. from the deep end wall for swimmers convenience.

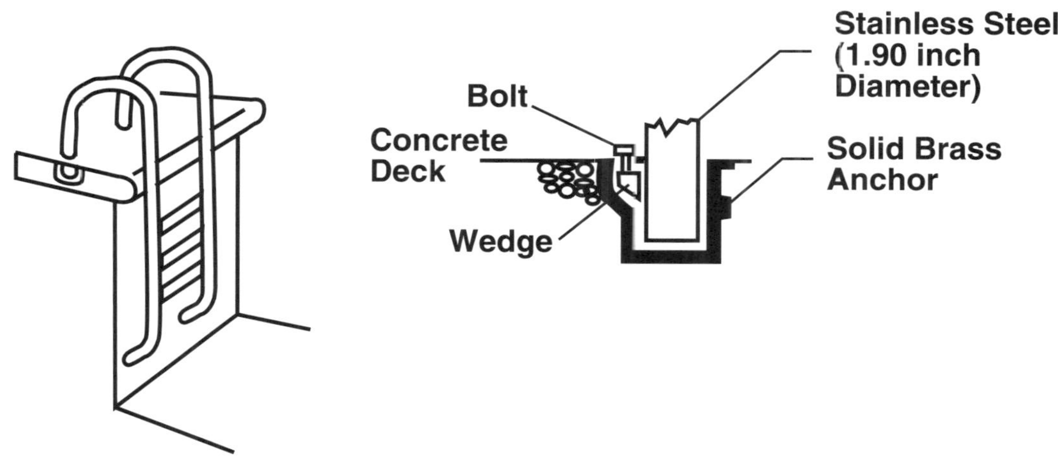

LADDERS/HANDRAILS

Handrails are available in many styles. The most popular are 36 and 40 inch, positioned on each side of the walk-in stairs. Handrails should be level and square to the pool shape. We mount them to brass anchors, like the ladders.

Other rails are mounted in the center of the stairs or diagonal to an inside stair.

Handrails greatly aid swimmers/bathers in entrance/exit to the swimming pool.

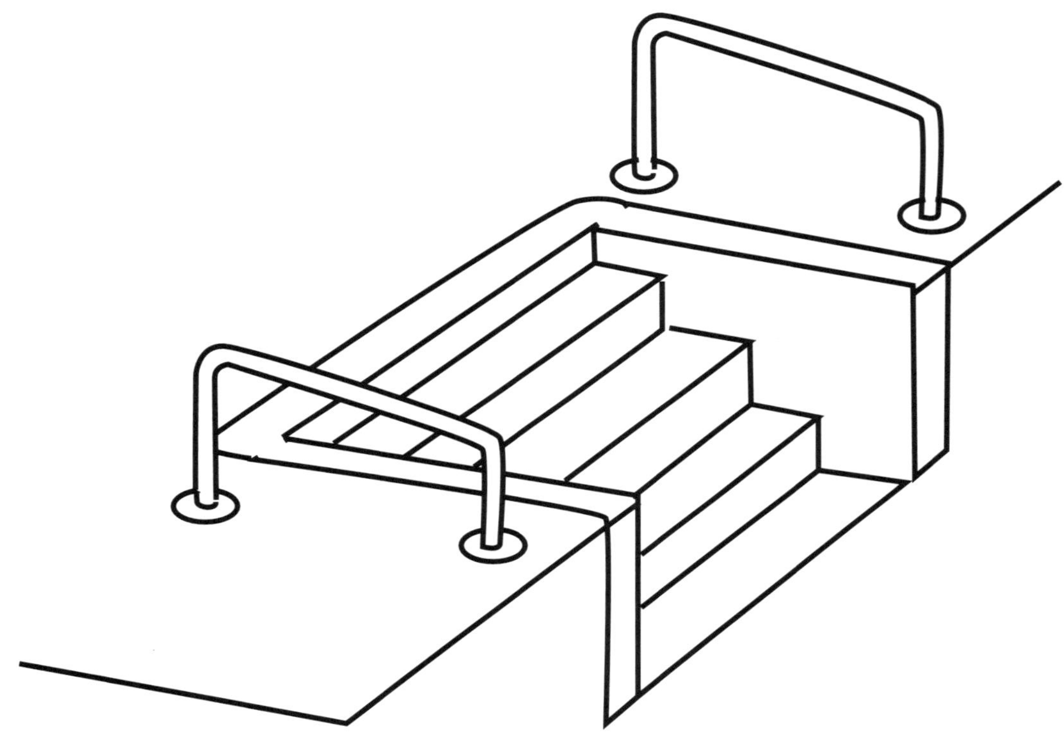

Constructing a new inground pool must be carefully considered and planned. First consider the location of all underground utilities:

1. **Electric/Phone**
   Usually located at your electric meter, connected to the power company outlet. Electric//phone lines are installed together in the same trench located a minimum of 36 inches below grade. For exact location contact Diggers Hotline, and the utility companies will locate these underground lines with orange paint/flags.

2. **Natural gas.**
   Located at the gas meter and installed toward the front of the home. Diggers Hotline will locate.

Once all utilities are located, consider any underground water systems:

Septic:
Septic lines and tank must be located and pinpointed to the exact location. Consult the local health department or contact the septic installer for septic site plans. Locate pool 25-30 ft. from septic tank and lines: that is code for some zoning departments: IMPORTANT: check with local zoning department for all building requirements.

Wells:
Wells should be a minimum of 15 ft. from the inside of pool walls. Again check with zoning department.

Home foundation drain tiles/land tiles:
Original building site plans should be examined to locate any under ground water systems, you must not disturb any of these waterways. Usually the sump pump outlet is located at the rear of the home. Make sure to install a pipe away from the pool area to avoid any problems later.

Flood zones:
Check with the county to make sure there are no flood zones running through the backyard.

When all utilities and underground water systems have been located , your swimming pool can be positioned to the best possible location. Consider two basic positions relative to the house with utilities, underground water systems and electric/gas lines located:

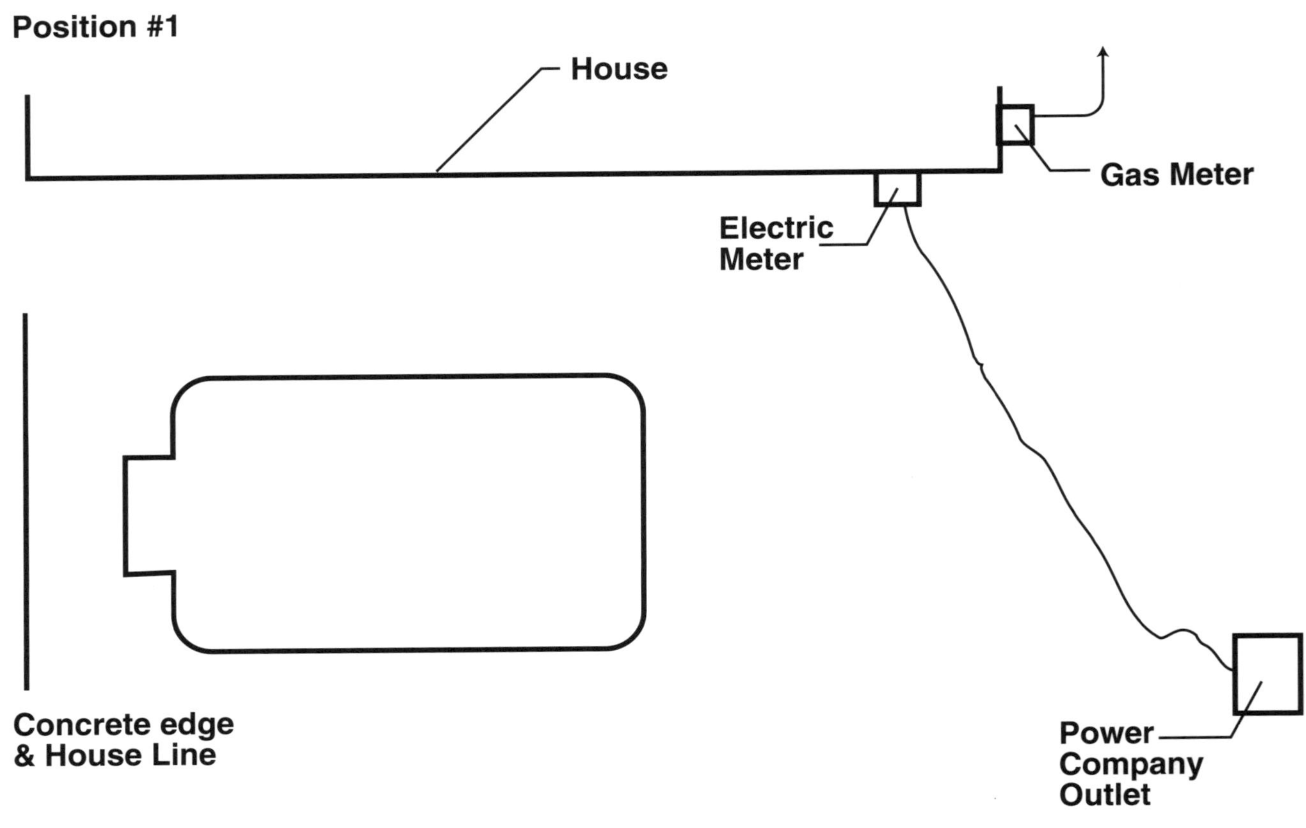
Position #1
House
Gas Meter
Electric Meter
Concrete edge & House Line
Power Company Outlet

Position #2

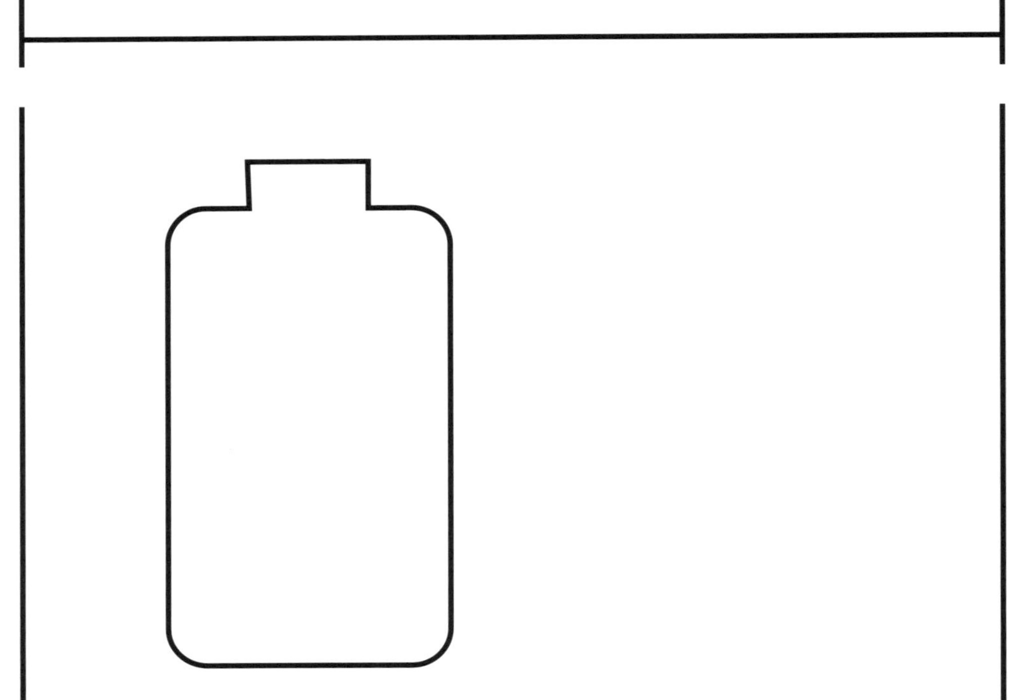

POSITION #1

This position is very popular. Its major advantage is an improved in-home view of the pool for added convenience. The pool area is located away from utilities to avoid additional expense. The pool deck is aligned with the house, coordinating it with the pool area. A control center is usually installed close to the house to reduce electric and gas hook-up costs. The filter, pump and heater are located at the control center. This position will help reduce building costs. For additional economy, an existing patio should be meshed to a new pool area. Patios are explained throughout the general text.

POSITION #2

This position is preferred for its configuration. Yard space is increased, providing additional room for a variety of recreational areas. The perpendicular position improves the appearance of the pool area. As above, the pool deck is aligned with the house. The control center is also located near the house on the pool side. A major advantage is an in-home view of the pool from one room; unlike position one, where you may have to enter three different rooms to view the pool. Construction costs are slightly higher.

INITIAL NOTES ____

Pool Grade Elevation

You have decided on a location for your new inground swimming pool. Now you must carefully decide on the pool grade height. If you're building fairly close to your home, as pictured, use the house grade level to determine pool grade height. Position the concrete level 2-4 inches below siding. This will give you a starting point to work from. Disregard any slope of land beyond the house and set grade level to house foundation/siding. If there is a slope, cut into and landscape appropriately; if no slope exists, fill low areas with gravel and raise land to pool grade height.

Also consider the concrete pitch. Pitch is .25 inches per ft.. For example: a four foot deck is pitched one inch lower to provide water run-off from the pool edge. With a new patio installation, pitch the concrete towards the pool deck and away from the center. Larger patios do not require as much pitch towards the pool decking. With an existing patio, set the pool concrete grade one inch above the patio end. (pool deck-4 ft. wide) Larger patios and pool decks require a drainage plate between them for improved water run-off. Normally, concrete pitch is sufficient to re-route splash and rain water.

Constructing a new inground pool is very messy and requires patience. A good time to build is in the fall. This way yard damage is minimized and usually money is saved on installation costs. After the pool is installed, black dirt and grass seed is spread to repair yard.

A new inground pool will completely change your yard into a functional fun area for many to enjoy. A new inground pool will increase your property value substantially. Your yard and new pool will become your focus and center of attention.

PITCH INCLUDED

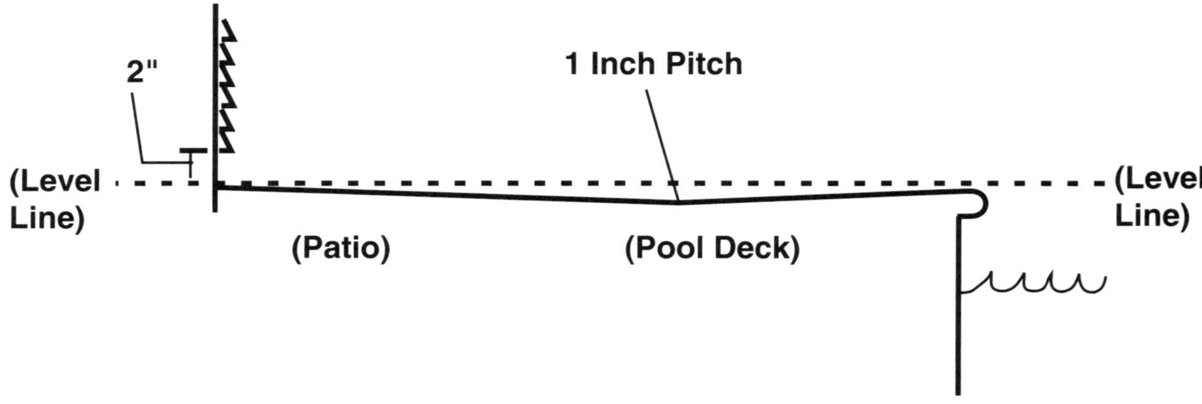

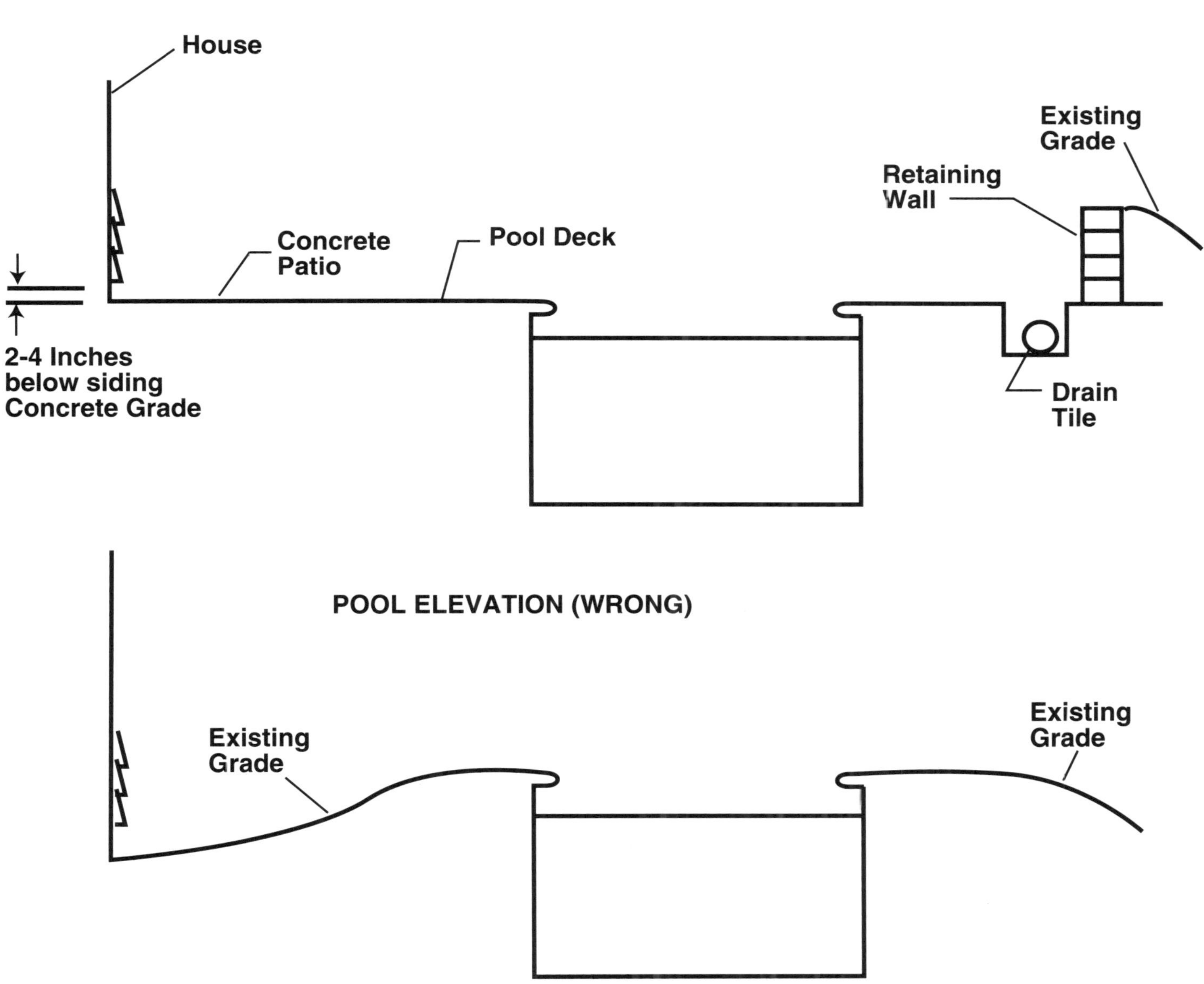
POOL ELEVATION (RIGHT)
House
Existing Grade
Retaining Wall
Concrete Patio
Pool Deck
2-4 Inches below siding Concrete Grade
Drain Tile
POOL ELEVATION (WRONG)
Existing Grade
Existing Grade

Retaining Walls

When facing a hill, excavate the elevation flat for pool and landscape area. Allow 4-6 ft. beyond concrete deck for retaining wall, landscaping and a drain tile. Tiles are installed to reroute any rain or splash pool water. They are positioned between the pool decking and the retaining wall.

It is very important to construct a retaining wall that will stand up to rain, snow and adverse weather conditions. Pour a concrete footing level and square, relative to the pool area. The retaining wall is then connected (sealed) and built upon the footing. Select from different wall materials:

1. **Brick**
2. **Gravity Blocks**
3. **Landscape Timbers**
4. **Railroad ties**

Brick walls are attractive and will last for many years. There are many styles and types of bricks to choose from. Only a footing is needed to support a brick wall. Gravity blocks are expensive, and can be troublesome to install and maintain. Weeds, grass and foliage will grow through the cracks after a period of time.

Landscape timbers

Landscape timbers are inexpensive and fun to work with when adding an adaptable, landscapeable pool area. Timbers are available in treated and non-treated lumber. Treated timbers are warranted for 30-40 years.

Railroad ties are commonly used because of their low cost. Ties must be properly installed to ensure a safe and secure pool area.

If the choice is made not to excavate into the hill, earth must be mounded up around the pool. This could cause settling problems later.

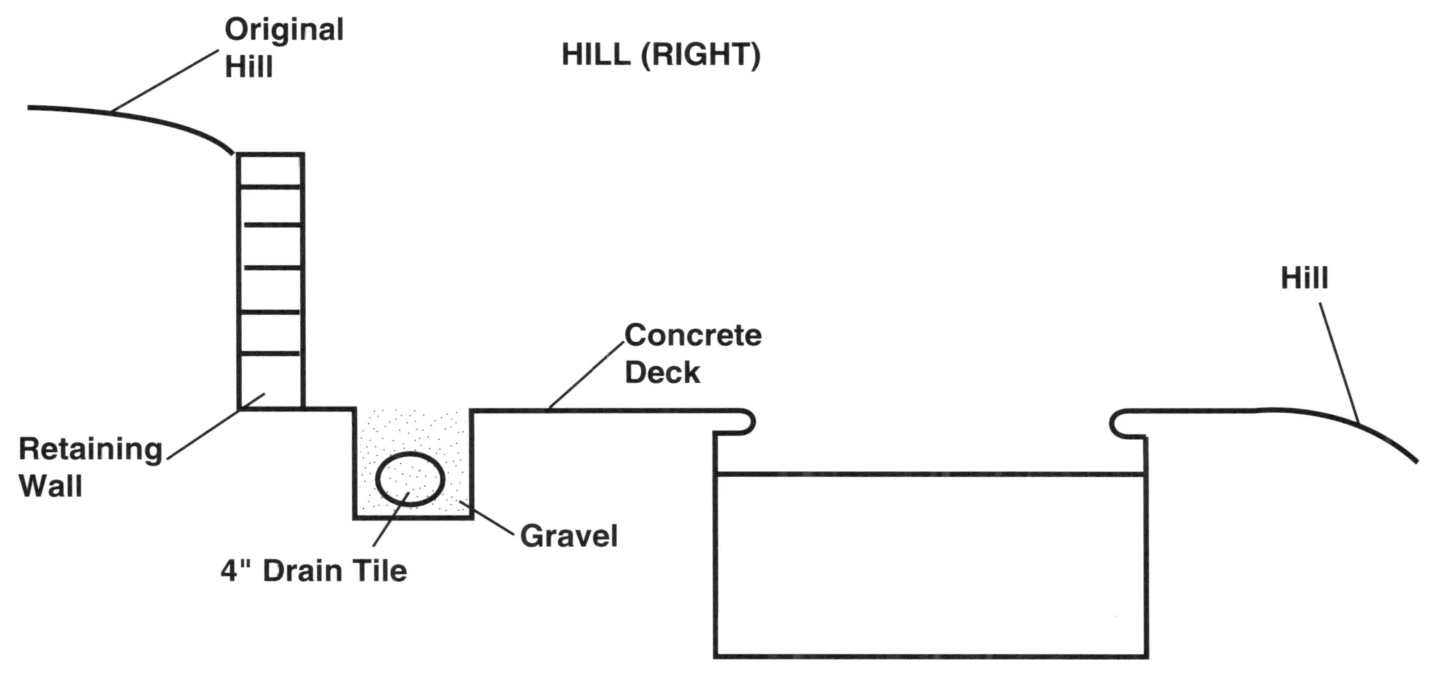
Original
Hill
HILL (RIGHT)
Hill
Concrete
Deck
Retaining
Wall
Gravel
4" Drain Tile

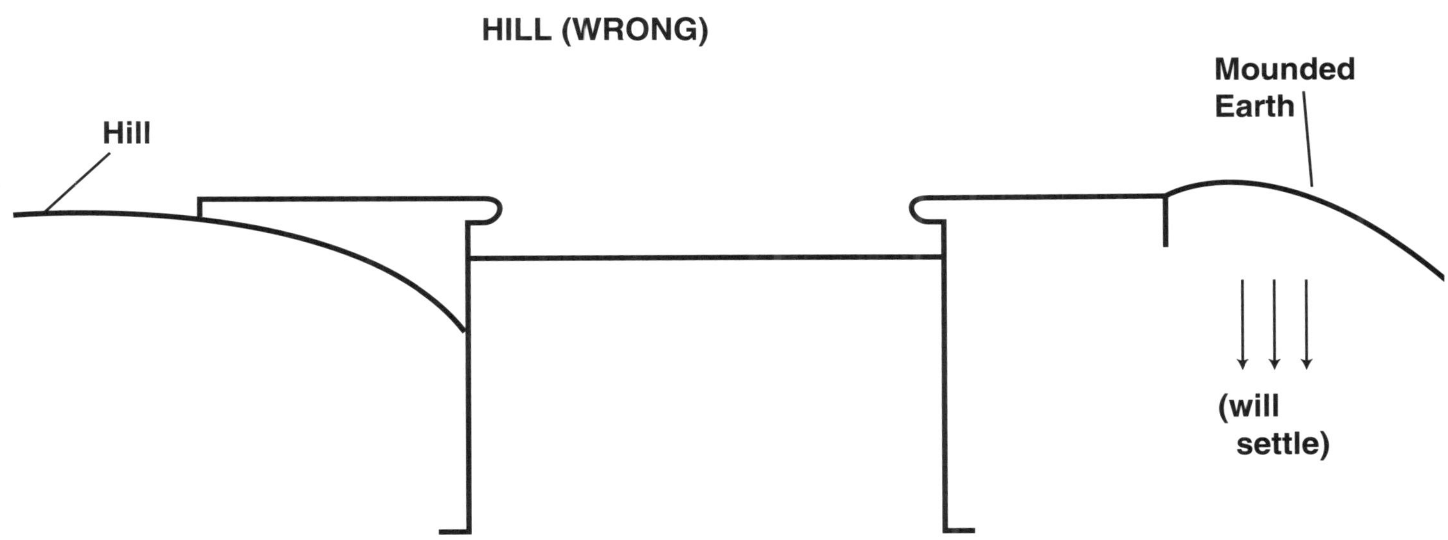
HILL (WRONG)
Mounded
Earth
Hill
(will
settle)

New Pool Design/Planning

You are ready to plan and design your new inground swimming pool. Visualizing the pool, concrete work and landscaping is your first task. Devise a plan on paper (site plan) to aid in the pool area layout. Actual staking will help you gain a feeling for the pool and surroundings. You must consider land elevations, dips, etc.. Here is a planning method for a 16 X 32 ft rectangle with 2 ft radius corners:

1. **Devise site plan (fig. 3)**
2. **Stake the actual pool dimensions (fig. 1)**
3. **Tie string to stakes**
4. **Paint ground**
5. **Stake pool concrete deck (fig. 2)**
6. **Tie strings, and paint**
7. **Locate fence**

Berms should be considered near the pool area. They are attractive and add privacy. They complement and enhance your yard. Berms are designed with topical drawings and organized hill structure. You can easily construct berms with extra earth taken from the pool site.

Four inch diameter drain tiles are positioned under berms to eliminate water build up and erosion. Then earth is dumped and shaped to a topical form. You can add trees, bushes and mulch for landscaping. I have devised a basic berm plan for you to follow: (fig. 4).

Control Centers

The control center is the filter/heater location: a concrete slab 4 x 8 ft, and 4 inches thick. Usually located next to the house for improved access, the control center is positioned near a rear door. You will spend time adding chlorine and maintaining equipment at the control center. Be sure to leave enough room at the control center so you are not crowded. (fig. 3)

NEW CONSTRUCTION

First, stake a rectangular 12 x 28 ft., and square to the house. Next, stake a radius at x1, then at x2, x3, and x4. Now, attach string and paint pool location:

FIG. 1

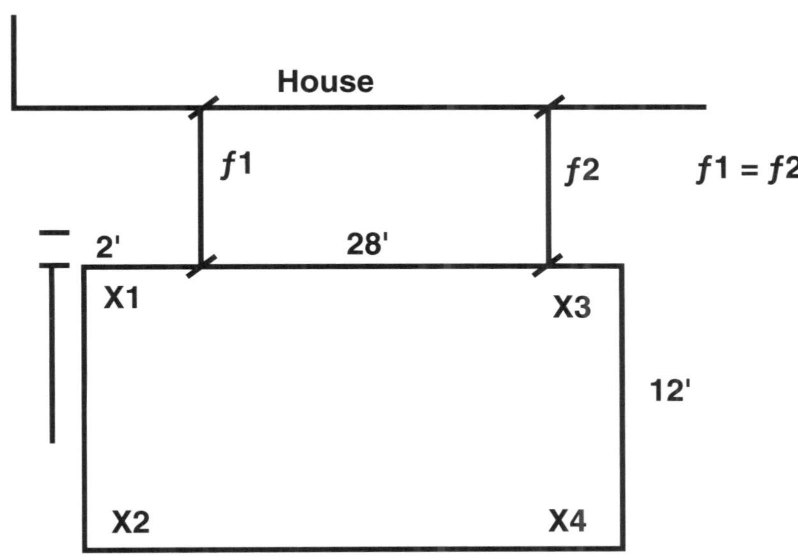

FIG. 2

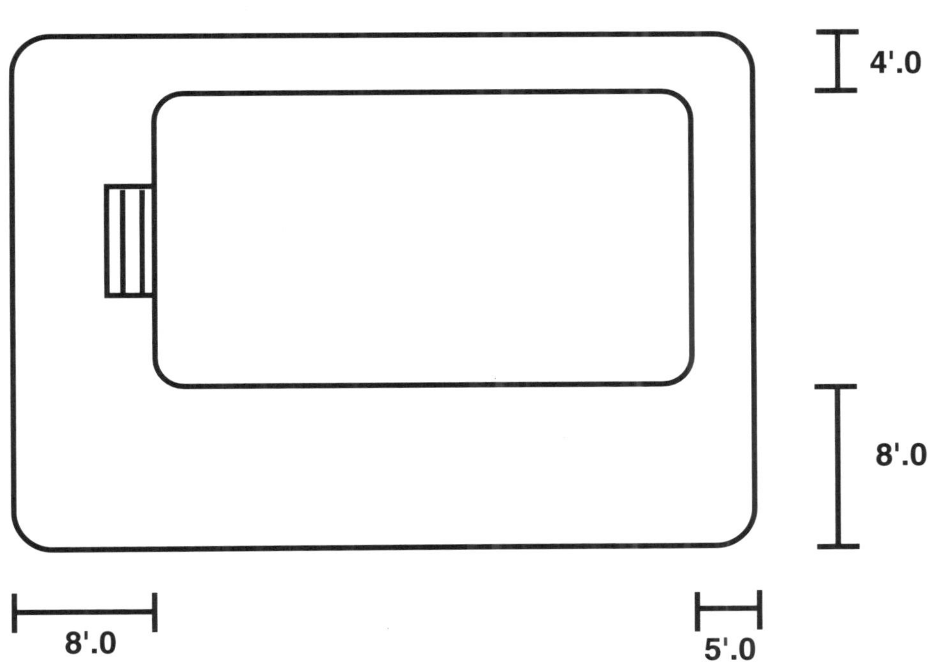

FIG. 3

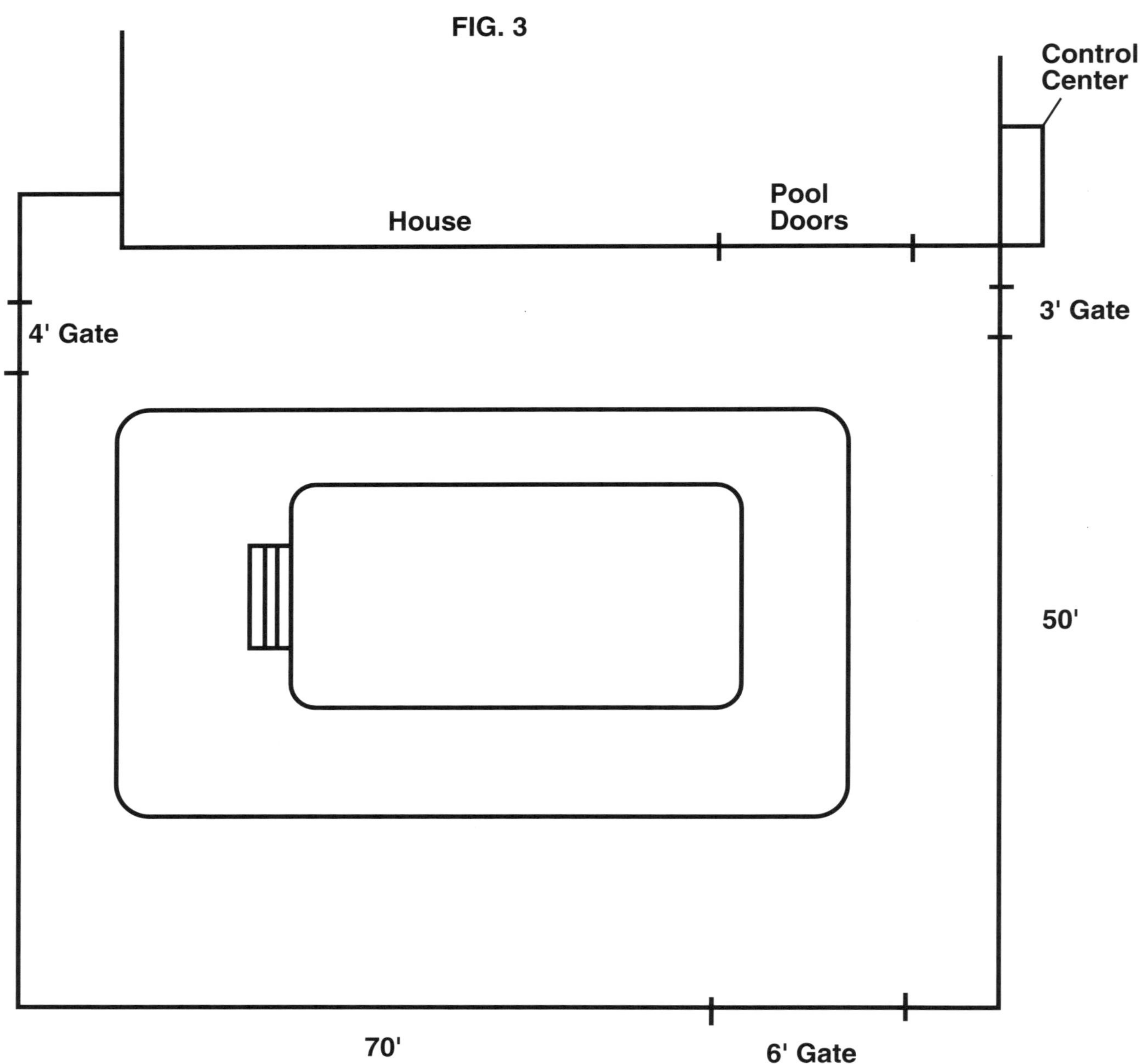

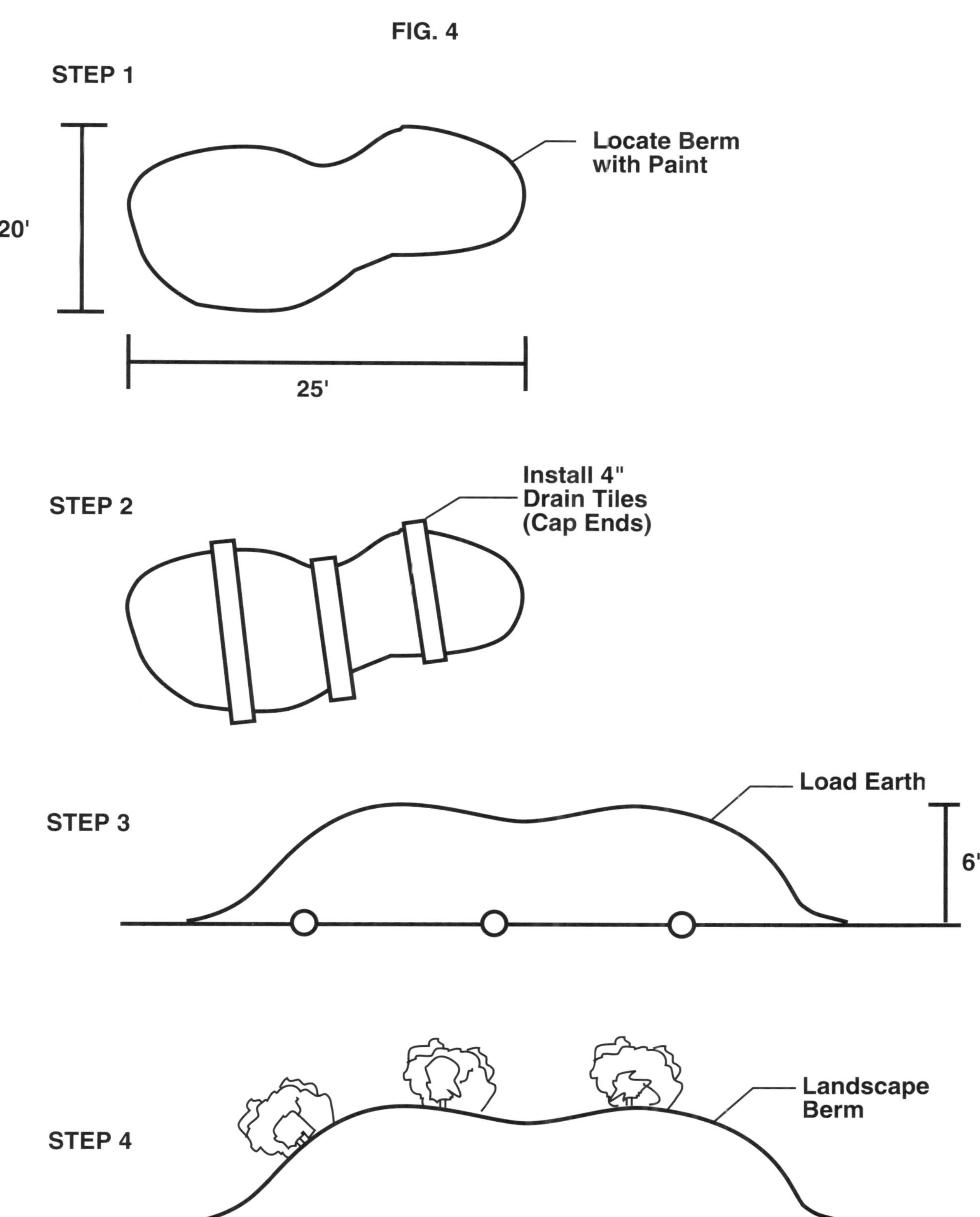
FIG. 4
STEP 1
20'
25'
Locate Berm with Paint
STEP 2
Install 4" Drain Tiles (Cap Ends)
STEP 3
Load Earth
6'
STEP 4
Landscape Berm

NEW CONSTRUCTION

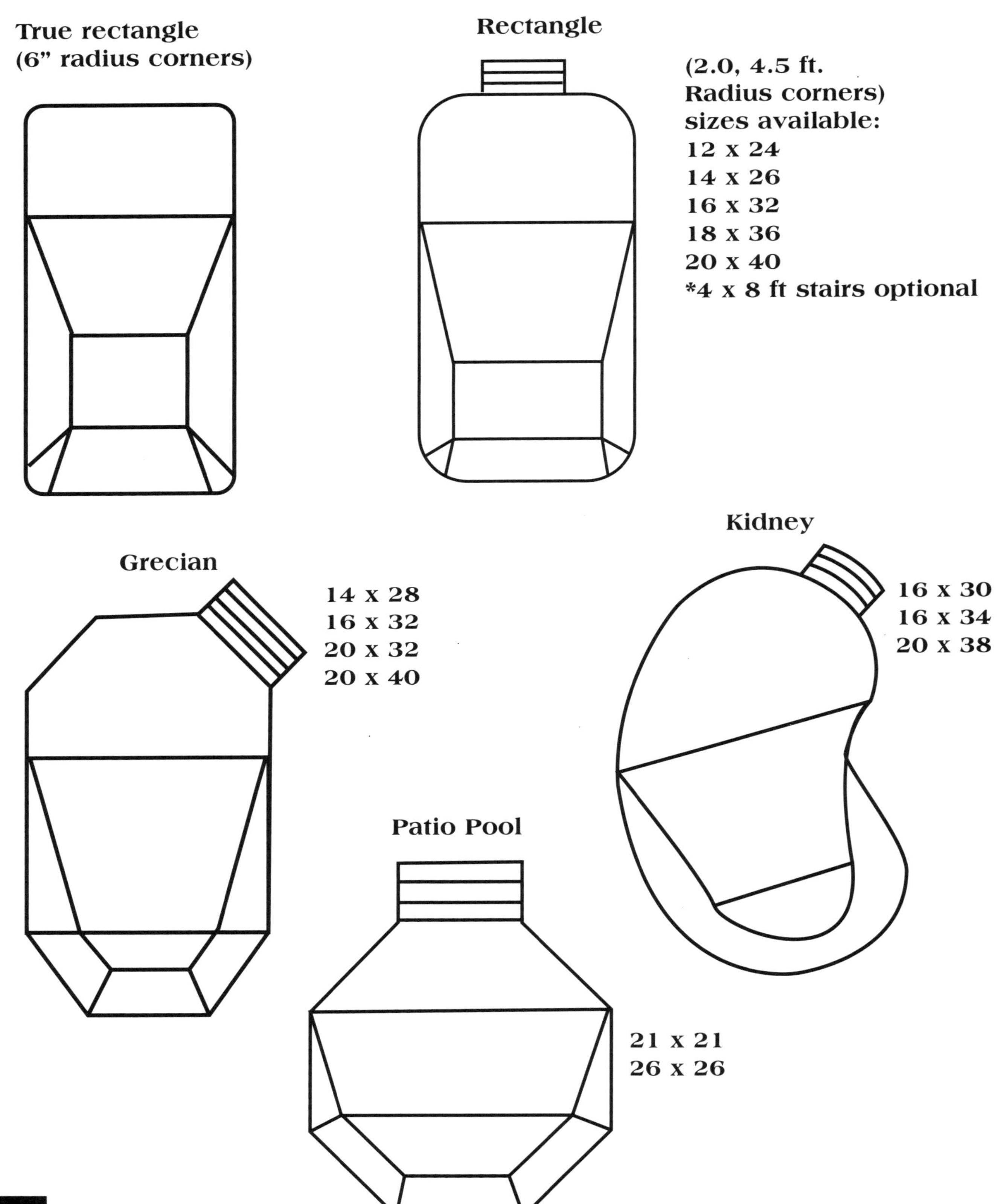

NEW CONSTRUCTION WORKSHEET

Pool Shape: ______________________________

Pool Size: ______________________________

Pool Type: ______________________________

Utilities: ______________________________

Electric/gas ______________________________

Phone ______________________________

Natural gas ______________________________

Diggers hotline (phone number): ______________________________

Septic system (yes) (no)

Location: ______________________________

Home water supply (well) (City)

Well Location: ______________________________

Sump pump (outlet) (yes) (no)

Location: ______________________________

Foundation Tiles (yes) (no)

Location: ______________________________

Flood zone (yes) (no)

Cable T.V. (yes) (no)

Location: ______________________________

Proposed pool position ______________________________

Pool grade elevation ______________________________

Retaining Wall (yes) (no)

Location: ______________________________

Berms (yes) (no)

Location: ______________________________

Control Center

Position ______________________________

Additional information: ______________________________

____

NOTES

CONCRETE POOLS

New Construction Plans

Concrete is a good solid structure: durable, and economical. Most houses and buildings are supported with a concrete foundation. Concrete is the most widely used building material for structures and solid bases. Concrete is chosen for strength and longevity.

Concrete pools can be used in any climate and will stand up to winter weather if properly installed and maintained. Many hotels and apartment complexes install concrete pools to save money. Gunite is an expensive concrete used for hotels, apartment complexes, etc.. Many people enclose concrete pools at their homes in northern climates, increasing the pool's life expectancy while decreasing repairs and maintenance.

Concrete pools can be very attractive and greatly increase the value of your home.

I have included the plans for a concrete pool, complete with optional whirlpool. I will discuss construction and provide a step-by step methodology. This pool can also be installed in a first class hotel.

Concrete used for swimming pools must be properly sealed to prevent deterioration from water. A good concrete silicone is used, preventing water-concrete contact. The area behind the walls is sealed with a water-proof primer and paint.

The concrete silicone film shown in fig. 4 acts as a seal and expansion/contraction area. This is a permanent unique safety seal which will last for years. It is designed to provide years of repair-free swimming. Most concrete pools do not include this feature.

Concrete pool shapes/sizes can be easily altered. Cuddle coves, whirlpools and slight overhanging concrete caps improve appearance and add a new functional design.

An addition may also be constructed. There is a chapter on additions, along with plans to construct.

Plans are attached for a 18 x 32 ft concrete pool. The following is construction methodology:

Excavation, Footing, Walls

Stake the rectangular pool with a 2 ft overdig (22 x 36 ft). Using a large backhoe, excavate the pool site: (9 inches below proposed finished bottom grade). Complete the excavation neatly and accurately.

Footings are then formed and poured with a 5 bag cement mixed concrete. Be sure to square footings to house. (fig. 1) Hand trowel footings and add a key hole. (fig. 2) As concrete is setting, install 1/2 inch rebar, (place on 2 ft. centers). After concrete is dry you must bond (ground) #8 copper wire to rebars and connect to a 8 ft ground rod. Wall forms are then installed and poured with a 5 bag mix concrete. You may pour a wider wall: 10 or 12 inches thick. Inlets, skimmers and light must be installed prior to wall concrete pour. Strip forms and pool walls are completed. You should grind form marks in the front of walls soon after concrete pour. Seal the back of walls with sprayed-on tar or sprayed epoxy primer and paint.

Note:

Pool excavation methods are explained in the pool excavation section. There are many tips mentioned to ensure a quality excavation.

Footings and walls can be poured with a stronger concrete to improve longevity. Shot-crete can be substituted to provide a more durable wall surface. The wall is very important. Special care and consideration should be taken. Shot-crete is a lot like Gunite, with superior properties. It can be ordered from many ready-mix companies. Regular 5-6 bag concrete may be used, and is encouraged. Concrete and construction methods are simplified in the concrete construction section.

Pool Bottom

The pool bottom must be evenly hand excavated to provide a constant thickness of concrete. Then form with wood stakes and nails (fig.3). Before pouring the pool base, install the main drain and 4 inches of pea-gravel.

IMPORTANT: Seal pool wall to bottom by applying concrete silicone to wall-footing area before pouring concrete, providing a seal that will last for years (fig.4). Level concrete, bowl float, and finish trowel concrete bottom.

IMPORTANT: Do not spray wet concrete surface with water to finish, this will weaken the concrete and will cause chipping and fracture.

Tile

Tile can now be installed at the water line. Use 4-8 rows of small tile. Use an attached tile pattern, install with frost-proof glue and frost-proof mortar.

Marcite

White marcite may be troweled on the walls and bottom. Apply an even coat with a pool trowel. The pool may be filled after marcite is completely cured. Complete underground plumbing and backfill with pea-stone. Now the concrete decking may be formed and poured. A precast cap must be installed prior to the pool deck installation.

Pre-cast cap

For improved appearance, a slightly overhanging square cap is preferred. Caps can be purchased at many concrete block plants. In fact, they can design and fabricate a special cap according to your specifications. A custom cap is decorative and affordable.

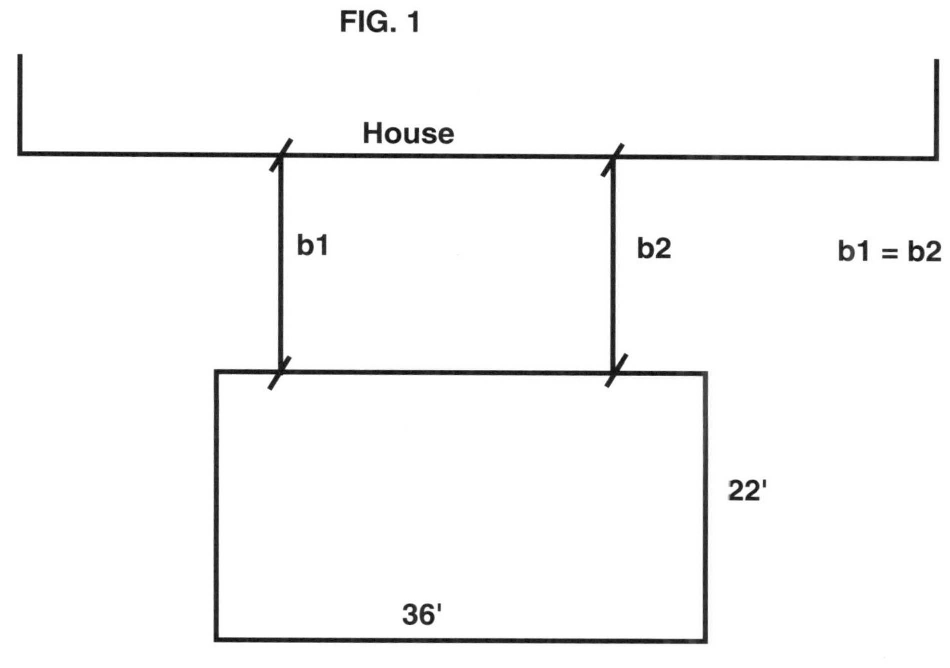
FIG. 1
House
b1
b2
b1 = b2
22'
36'

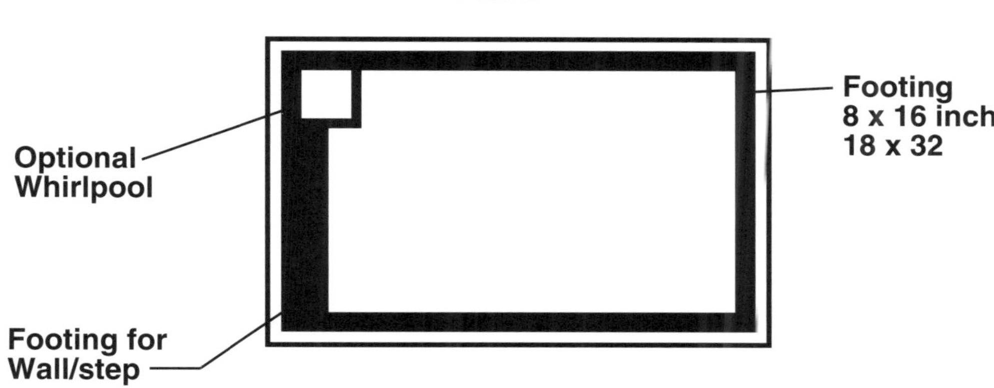
FIG. 2
Footing
8 x 16 inch
18 x 32
Optional
Whirlpool
Footing for
Wall/step

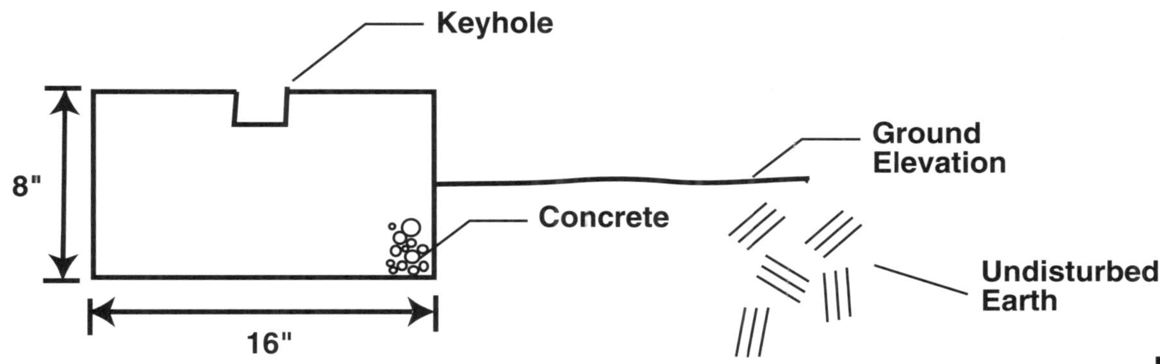
Keyhole
Ground
Elevation
8"
Concrete
Undisturbed
Earth
16"

FIG. 3

Steel Bar
Concrete
Leveling Board
Wood Stakes
with Pins
Steel Bar
Pins
Concrete
Surface
9"
5 inches of concrete
4 inches of pea gravel
Undisturbed
Earth

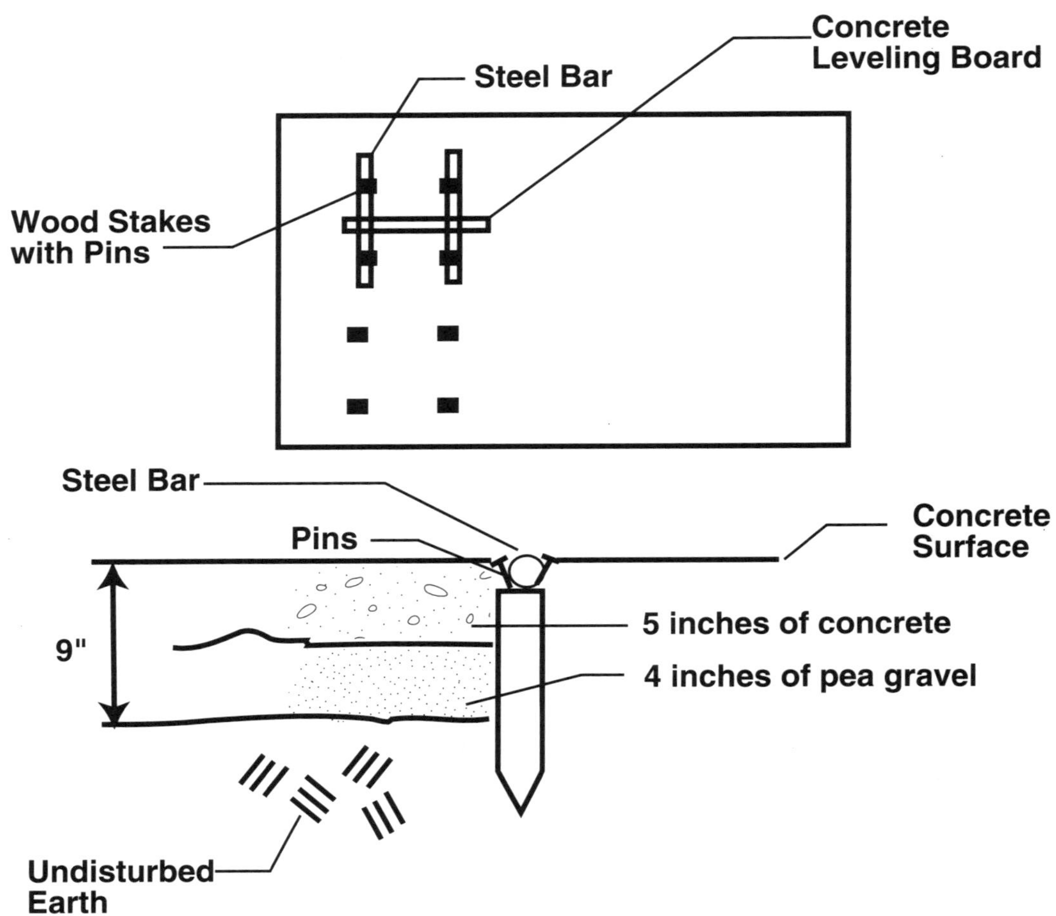

FIG. 4

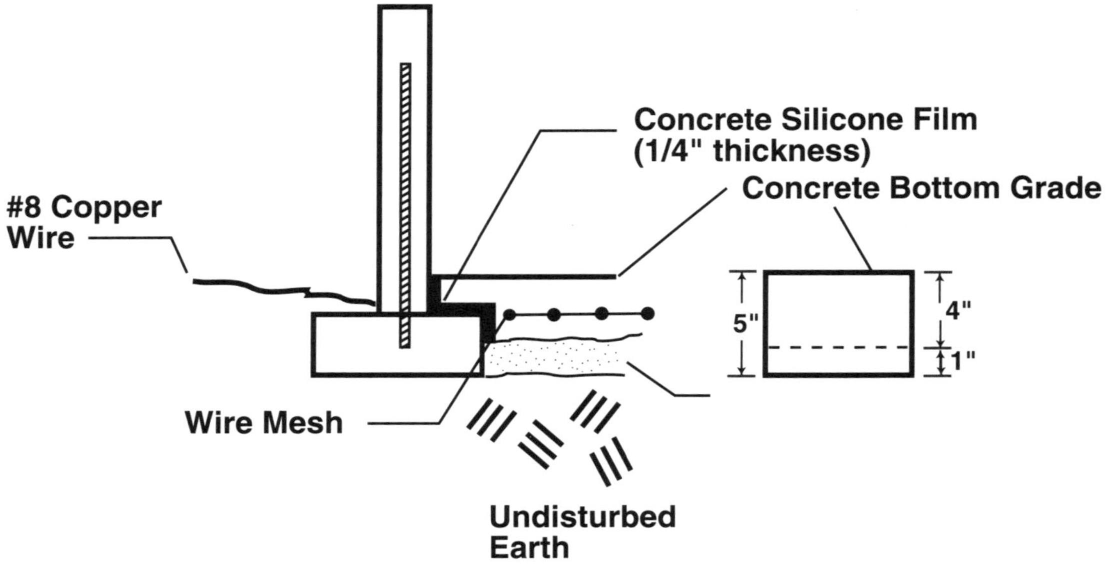

Concrete Silicone Film
(1/4" thickness)
Concrete Bottom Grade
#8 Copper
Wire
5"
4"
1"
Wire Mesh
Undisturbed
Earth

Maindrain/Hydrostatic Valve

The maindrain must be installed with a hydro-valve to prevent ground water pressure from building up under the concrete bottom. The valve will allow ground water to enter the pool if the pressure is too excessive.

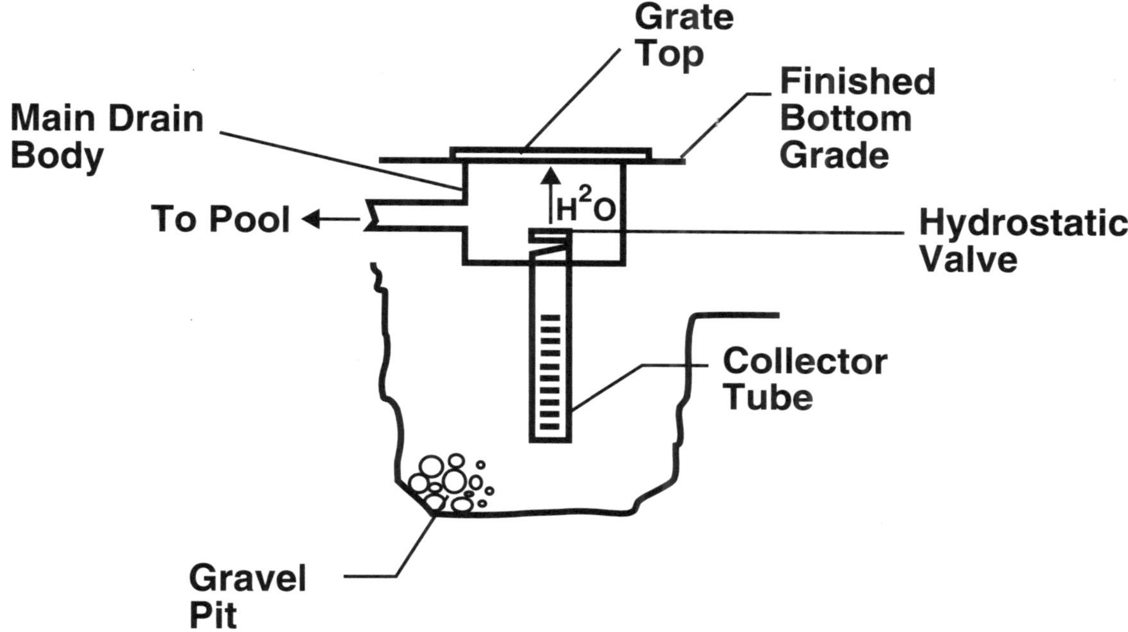

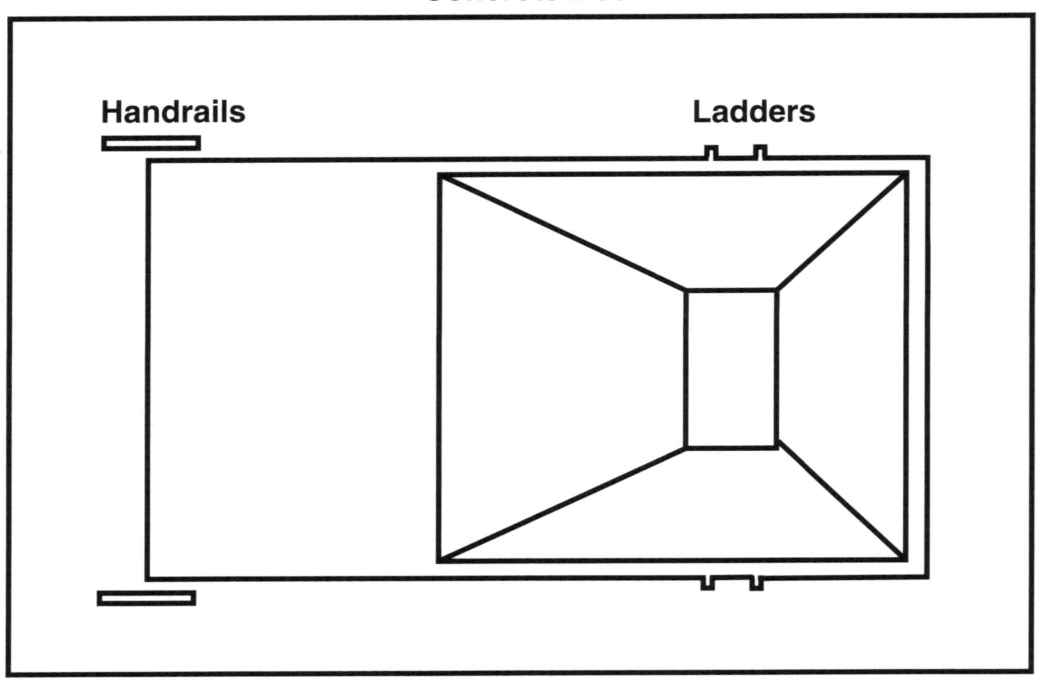

POOL DATA:
Size: 18 x 32 ft.
Depth: 6 ft.
Capacity: 28,000 gal.
Perimeter: 100 ft.

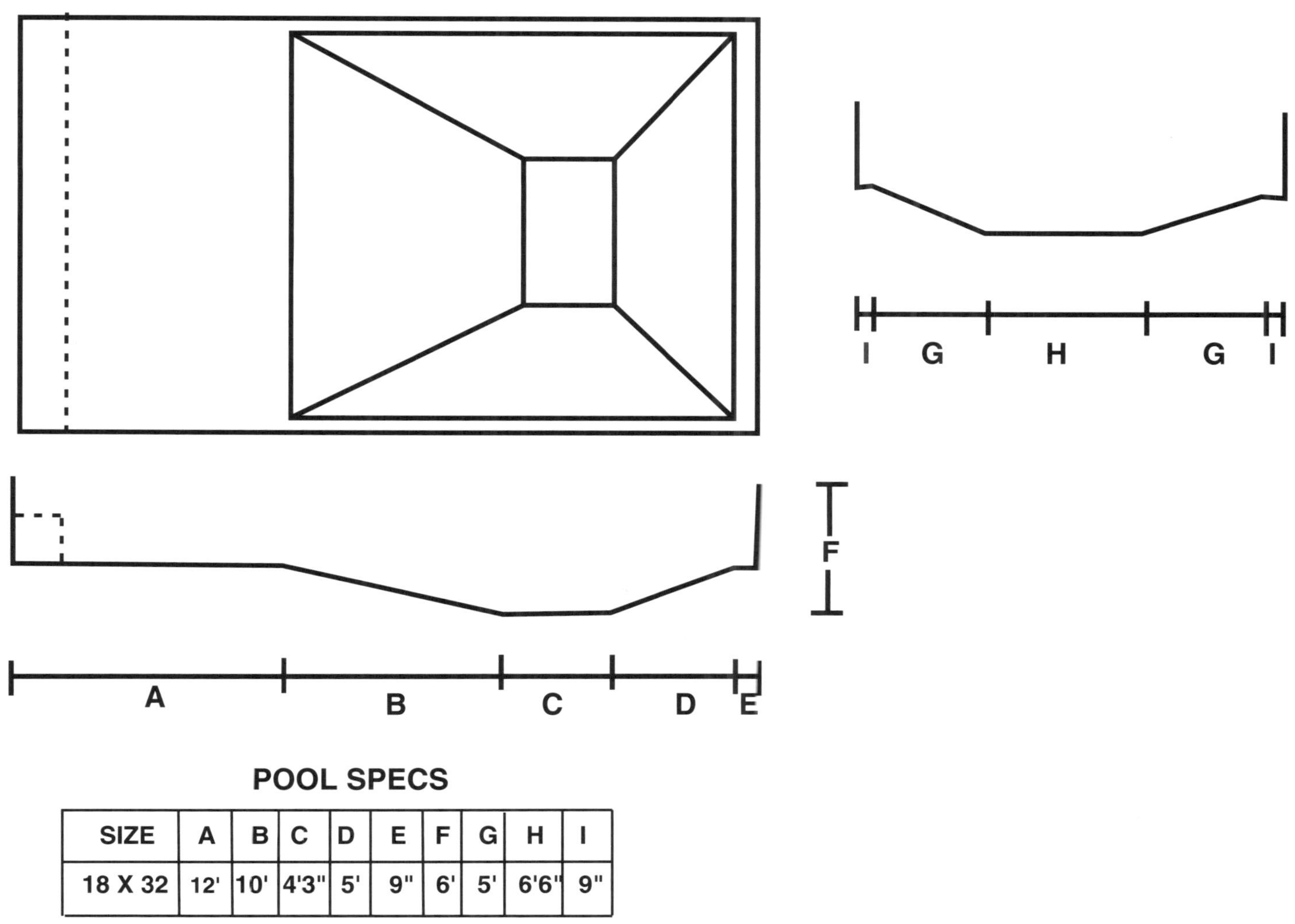

POOL SPECS

SIZE	A	B	C	D	E	F	G	H	I
18 X 32	12'	10'	4'3"	5'	9"	6'	5'	6'6"	9"

Note: Safety ledge can be omitted.

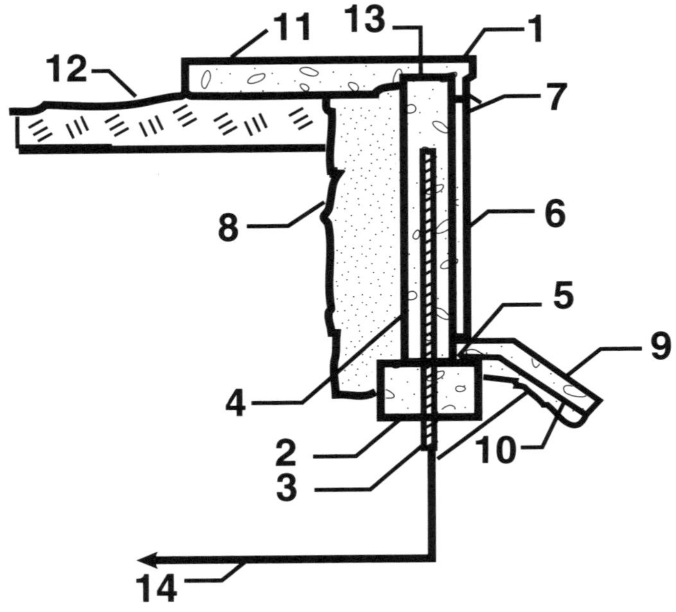

STRUCTURAL DETAIL

1. Cap: Pre-Cast Concrete
2. Footing ' 8 x16 in. 5 Bag concrete mix
3. Rebar ' 1/2 in. dia. - 2 ft. centers
4. Wall ' 8 x 48 in. 5 Bag concrete mix
5. Seal Concrete silicone film (1/4" thickness)
6. Marcite Pool finish
7. Tile Frost proof with grout
8. Pea gravel: backfill
9. Floor ' 5 in. thickness (5-6) bag mix
10. Wire mesh ' (6 x6) in. x 10 gauge
11. Deck ' Concrete (6) bag mix
12. Undisturbed earth
13. Sealed joint ' 1.5 in. polyurethane capped with mortar
14. #8 solid copper ground wire ' all rebar and wire mesh to be connected to a ground rod

WHIRLPOOLS/SPA PLANS

A whirlpool can be incorporated into a swimming pool design. A fully functional spa near the pool is practical. The pool's filter/heater can be used to operate the nearby spa, but since the cost is minimal, separate equipment should be purchased.

There are several types of whirlpools. The following are three different construction materials:

1. **Fiberglass/acrylic shell**
2. **Poured concrete walls/bottom**
3. **Gunite/Marcite**

Fiberglass/Acrylic is the most popular and widely used. The shell is attractive and comfortable. Larger shells are expensive. An inexpensive alternative is a poured concrete whirlpool. I have included plans for an 8 x 8 ft. spa.

Fiberglass/Acrylic is available in many colors: white, gray, blue, red, etc.. The shell is coated with an insulating foam. Inlet and skimmer holes are molded or cut-in. Extreme care must be taken in handling a one-piece shell so that the interior surface is not scratched or damaged. Installation is usually indoors because adverse weather conditions may cause damage to the spa and its operating equipment. A spa room in the basement or upstairs is practical.

Concrete poured walls/bottom is a very inexpensive way to construct a larger spa. These whirlpools feature a real tile border, white marcite bottom/sides and a slight overhanging precast cap similar to spas at major hotels. This spa can be any shape or size. This design can be turned into a small swimming area as well: a swim-spa. On the following page are the plans for an 8 x 8 ft spa, with enough room for occupation by eight people comfortably.

Gunite/marcite spas look a lot like poured concrete spas. They include tile border, flowing bottom contour and tile caps. Larger hotel spas are usually gunite design; built for strength and designed for a pleasurable whirlpool area.

First, consider spa functions.

Whirlpools (spas) function a lot like inground swimming pools. The water is both filtered and heated. A lot of pump power is required to successfully run the inlets (jets).

All spas use a cartridge filter system because they are efficient and the water capacity to be filtered is usually 200-500 gallons. You must clean the filter periodically.

Heating a spa is a lot different than heating an inground swimming pool. An in-line heater will heat the water very slowly in conjunction with a heavy duty spa-cover. The spa will always be covered to trap valuable heat. In fact, the cover actually heats the pool.

The in-line heater warms the water 1-2 degrees per hour. Because the heat is trapped by the cover the spa continues to heat. Without the cover, the water will not reach optimum temperature. With the cover, it continues to heat until the temperature reaches approximately 100 degrees. A thermostat can be used to adjust spa temperature. If the spa is used sparingly, heat only before the intended use. This is a money saving practice. Spa pump motors usually have two speeds:

1. Filtering/heating (LOW)
2. Jet Inlets (HIGH)

The filter/heating low speed is frequently used. The high speed is only needed when the spa is in use. Two speed pumps are a good way to operate a spa. Consider installing a powerful 2-3 HP. pump to operate the jets.

Air bubbles are generated from an air-blower. Blowers usually connect to an air-system located in the floor of the spa. Blowers are inexpensive and available in 1-2 HP...

The spa jet inlets are injected with air from tubes connected to above the water control valve, usually located near the spa controls. Just loosen the control knob and air is supplied to each inlet.

The whirlpool plans can be easily constructed from the concrete pool section. Simply follow the same procedure for footings, walls and bottom, along with methods for tile, marcite, pre-cast cap and decking. (Refer to the concrete pool section.)

WHIRLPOOL/SPA PLANS

8 Ft.
8 Ft.
4.0'
1.5'
5.0'
1.5'

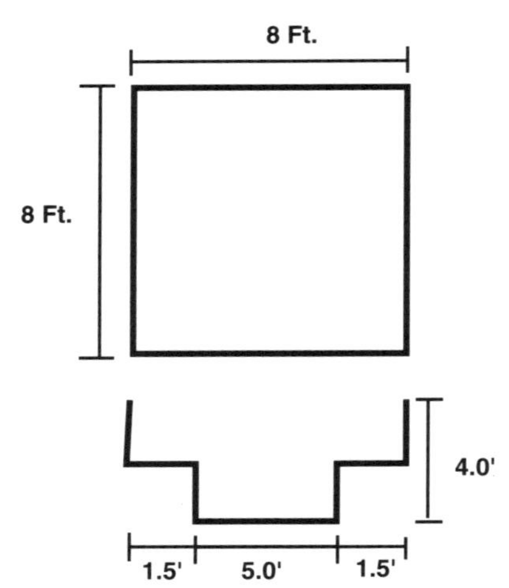

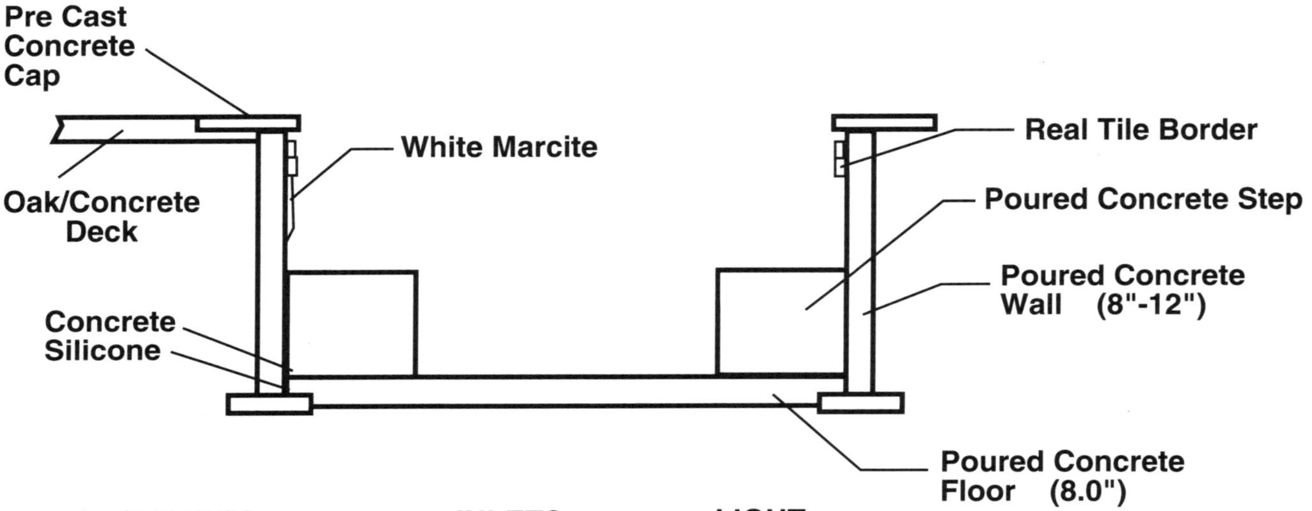

Pre Cast Concrete Cap
Oak/Concrete Deck
White Marcite
Real Tile Border
Poured Concrete Step
Poured Concrete Wall (8"-12")
Concrete Silicone
Poured Concrete Floor (8.0")

SKIMMER

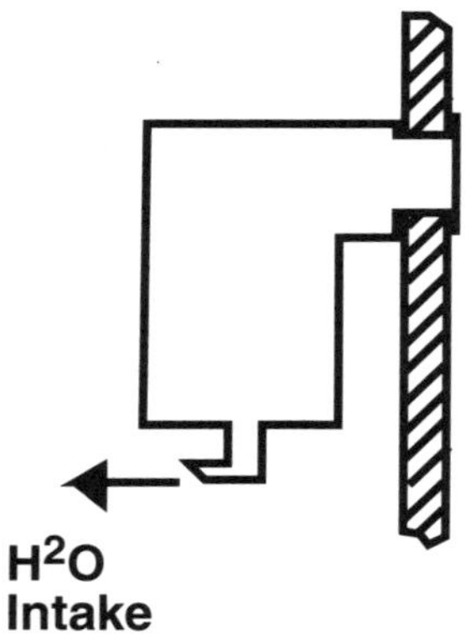

H^2O Intake

INLETS

H^2O Return

LIGHT

12 Volt

MAINDRAIN

Air
H^2O Intake
Air Blower Pipe

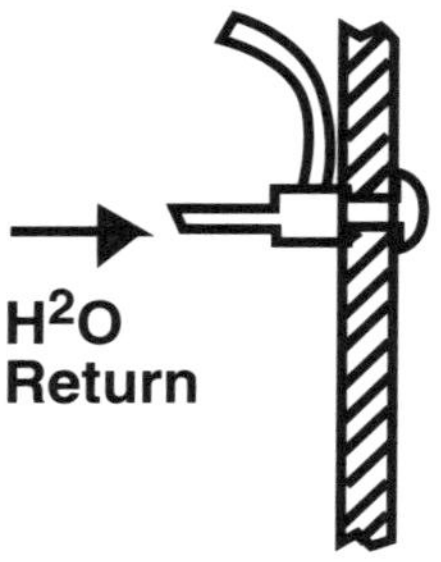

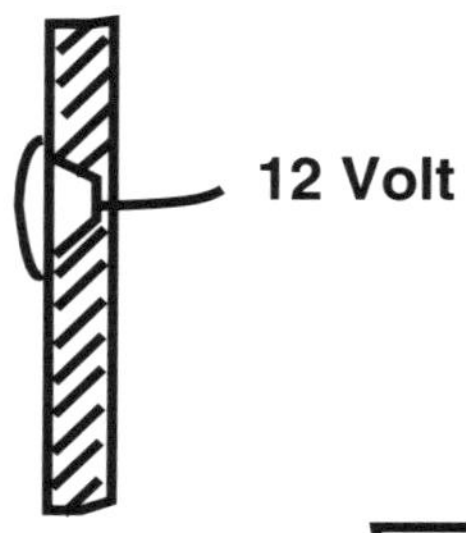

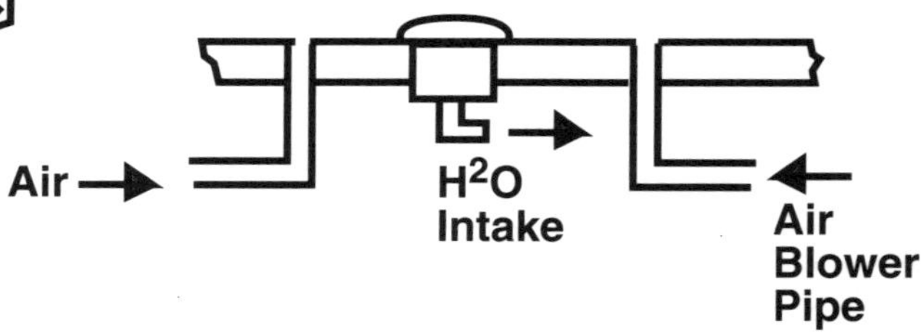

ADDITIONS/INDOOR POOLS

Pools enclosed in a building/addition complement your existing home and increase the value. You can build an inexpensive addition that is good enough for any home. Included are plans and design for an addition suitable for an inground pool. Some of the features are: vaulted ceilings, large 4 x 6 ft. windows; a separate utility room, cedar interior, exterior, sunroofs, recessed lighting, etc..

Construction begins with a standard foundation. Usually the pool installation is coordinated with the addition. The following are details of construction methodology, humidity, water cleaning and chemistry.

Humidity is present at all times. When designing a suitable addition humidity resisting components must be implemented. Proper air circulation is required. There are two methods mentioned.

The first method is to install an air dryer, converting warm humid air into dry hot air. This is somewhat expensive, but it is the best way to eliminate humidity.

Another method is to ventilate the pool area with vent fans, utilizing a regular natural gas furnace; 80-120,000 BTU, and installing a central switch to maintain humidity at a constant 40%. Humidity is then vented automatically. The initial cost is low but the operation is more expensive. This method requires a solar cover on the pool surface.

Constructing the addition frame with treated wood will resist and hold up to humidity. The key is to eliminate humidity before it reaches the frame and rafters. Framing, rafters, and waterproof interior are installed. Waterproof drywall should be used, and sealed with epoxy paint. Tongue and groove cedar can be installed, insulating and absorbing excess humidity, and adding a decorative functional interior.

A cedar interior and exterior are not absolutely necessary. Substantial savings can be realized by using a cedar substitute on the exterior. Waterproof drywall can be installed in the interior. Cedar is somewhat expensive but careful planning can aid in reducing design and construction costs.

Recessed lights are sealed and protected, providing adequate visibility. These lights are inexpensive and require little maintenance. Wiring is easy, consisting of two ground fault breakers.

Large 4 x 6 ft windows spaced evenly on sides and ends provide outside viewing. Double pane glass insulates and protects them from winter weather conditions.

Sunroofs are installed to light the pool area during the daytime. Sunrays are trapped and aid in additional heating, acting as a passive solar system. Sunroofs require vaulted ceiling installation.

Vaulted ceilings increase pool area and provide an improved decor.

The enclosed pool remains cleaner because of the absence of trees, bushes, bugs, etc.. Enclosed pools require less maintenance; however, the pool water must still be filtered.

Bromine or chlorine can be used to treat water, but Bromine is preferred because of decreased chemical dissipation. Most indoor pools are poured concrete walls/bottom, and Bromine is preferred for use in this type of pool. An in-line Bromine feeder is installed at the filter/heater.

A heater installed in the utility room will aid in addition heating. An in-wall fan can be added to distribute excess heat from the pool heater. Depending on the heater size, it is surprising how much heat can be generated.

This particular addition is designed to provide a lot of light from outside and viewing from inside. A good selection of accessories have been added to decrease heating bills, improve lighting and increase swimming conditions.

Following is a detailed design and plans for an addition including an inground swimming pool. The pool is excavated, then the addition is erected. Plans and construction methodology are included in the concrete pool section.

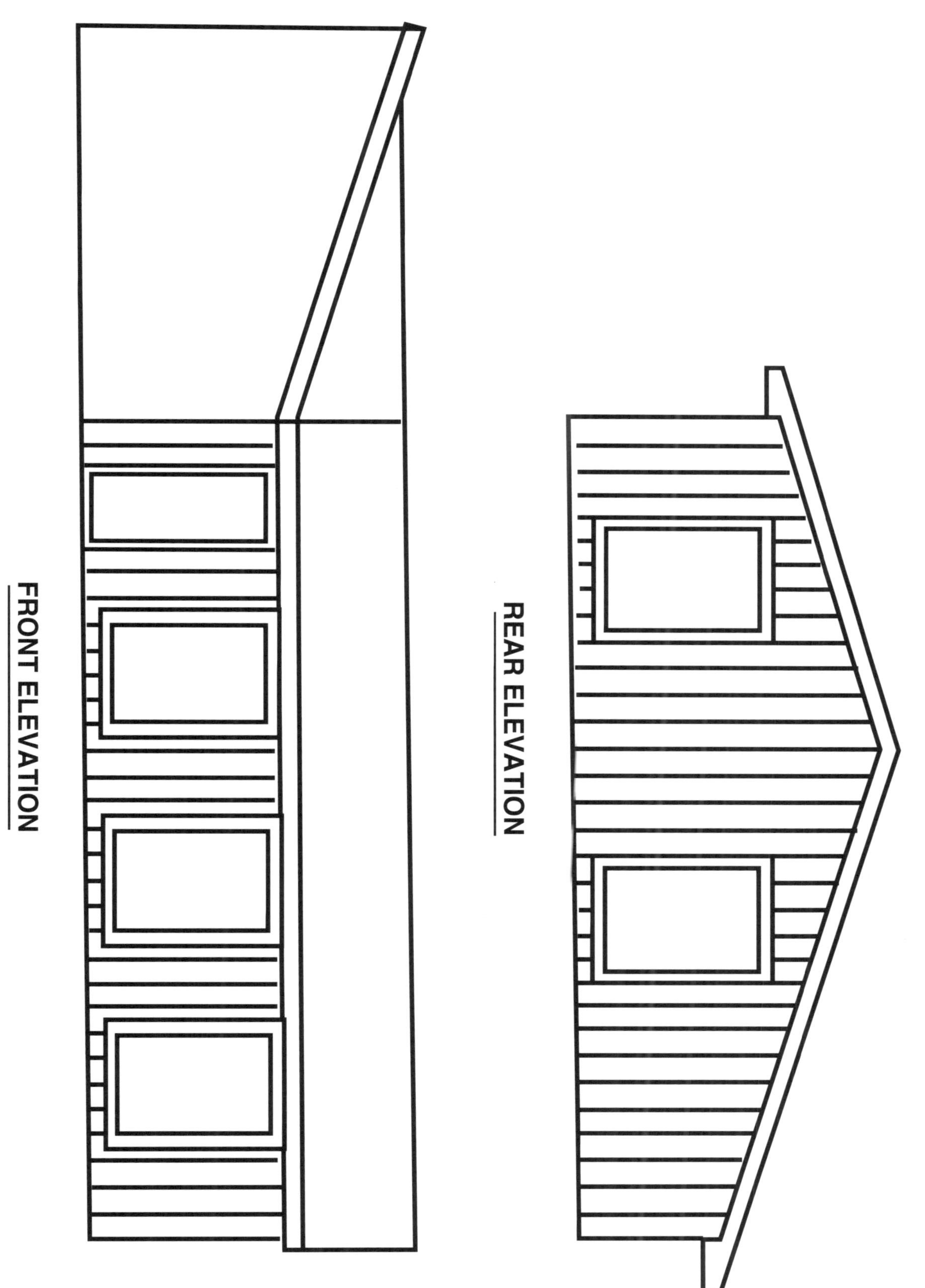
FRONT ELEVATION
REAR ELEVATION

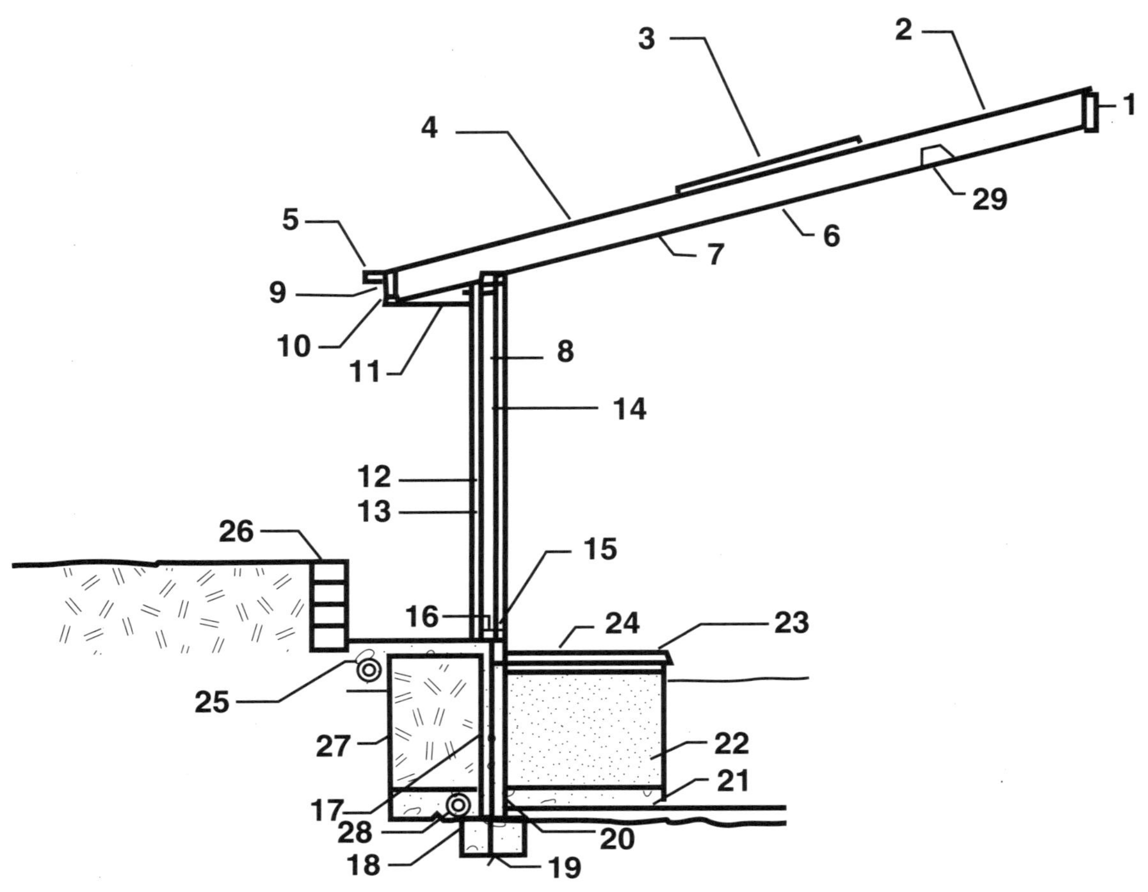

CROSS SECTION 3/8"=1 ft.

1. Ridge Board (2x10 inch)
2. Plywood (3-ply X-1/2 inch thickness)
3. Skylight (22-1/2 x 46 1/2)
4. Shingles: Fiberglass with 15 lb. Felt
5. Gutters
6. Drywall: Waterproof (1/2 inch thick)
7. Wood Rafters 2 x 8 inch on 16 inch center
8. Walls: wood 2 x 4 inch
9. Fascia: wood 1 x 3 inch
10. Sub-Fascia 2 x 6 inch
11. Vents: Aluminum (3 x 16 inch on 8 ft. center)
12. Celotex (1/2 inch)
13. Cedar siding
14. Insulation: 3-11/3.5 inch
15. Sill: 2 x 4 inch treated Lumber with foam sealer
16. Concrete Bolts
17. Tar
18. Concrete Footing: 1.33 x .67 ft = 5 bag mix
19. Rebar: 3/8 inch 5 ft o.c.
20. Concrete Wall: .67 X 4 ft : 5 bag mix
21. Pool concrete footing 6-10 inch
22. Pea stone backfill
23. Concrete deck (4 inch thick)
24. Rebar: 1/2 inch diameter (4 ft c.c.)
25. Tile Drainage System, Pitch; 1/4 inch/ft.
26. Gravity block retraining wall
27. Earth backfill
28. Drainage Tile
29. Recessed Light

Ponds are attractive and will complement any outdoor setting. Landscaping can include Lanin Stone, berms, statues, bushes, trees and mulch. Water fountains, waterfalls, etc. can also be added.

Because ponds are free form, they can be any shape or size.
The following are plans for a concrete pond, size: 20 x 25 ft.. To begin with, ponds should be excavated with a small backhoe to a depth of at least 2' 6", and the earth relocated. This depth will accommodate suitable living conditions for goldfish, frogs and underwater plant life. Algae growth is common and can be cleaned periodically with special water additives that can be purchased from most stores. Small pumps and filters can be added to ensure clear, clean water.

The following is a basic pond design. The plans can be altered as needed.

CONSTRUCTION

1. Draw a site plan as your guide. Include the pond location, landscaping, lights, fountains, etc.. Stake the location with string and paint. Allow 12 inches for working room at the pond perimeter.

2. Excavate the pond site to a depth of at least 2' 6" and set aside the topsoil and underlying earth for landscaping. Set concrete forms (flexible boards) to the curvature of the pond one foot inside the excavated perimeter.

3. Add 4 inches of pea gravel for a suitable concrete base. (Refer to the section on concrete construction). Lay wire mesh and set steel rebar stakes 5-6 inches above pea gravel at intervals to ensure uniform thickness and pour 5-6 inches of patio mix concrete. Rough trowel and finish. Let concrete cure 4-5 days. Apply epoxy-based primer. A hand-held roller works very well for this application. Let cure and apply the second coat, black pool paint.

4. Add earth, topsoil and landscape as desired. Stack Lanin Stone or Flagstone at pond perimeter. Then add trees, bushes and mulch according to your landscape plan.

PONDS

PROCEDURE

1. Stake pond location.

2. Excavate pond site.

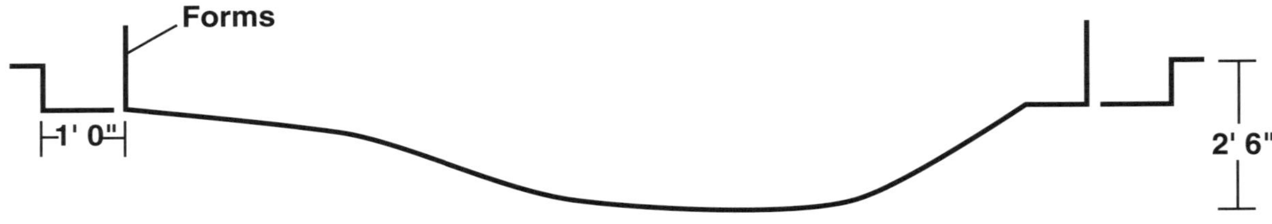

3. Set concrete forms. (level)

4. Install pea gravel and grade pins, pour concrete.
(Be sure to remove grade pins as you pour concrete)

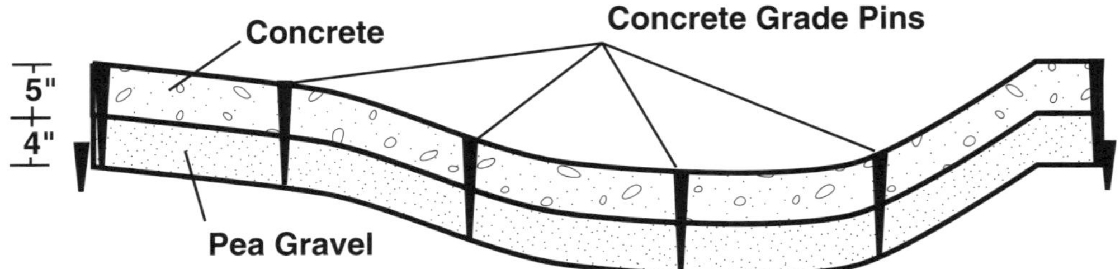

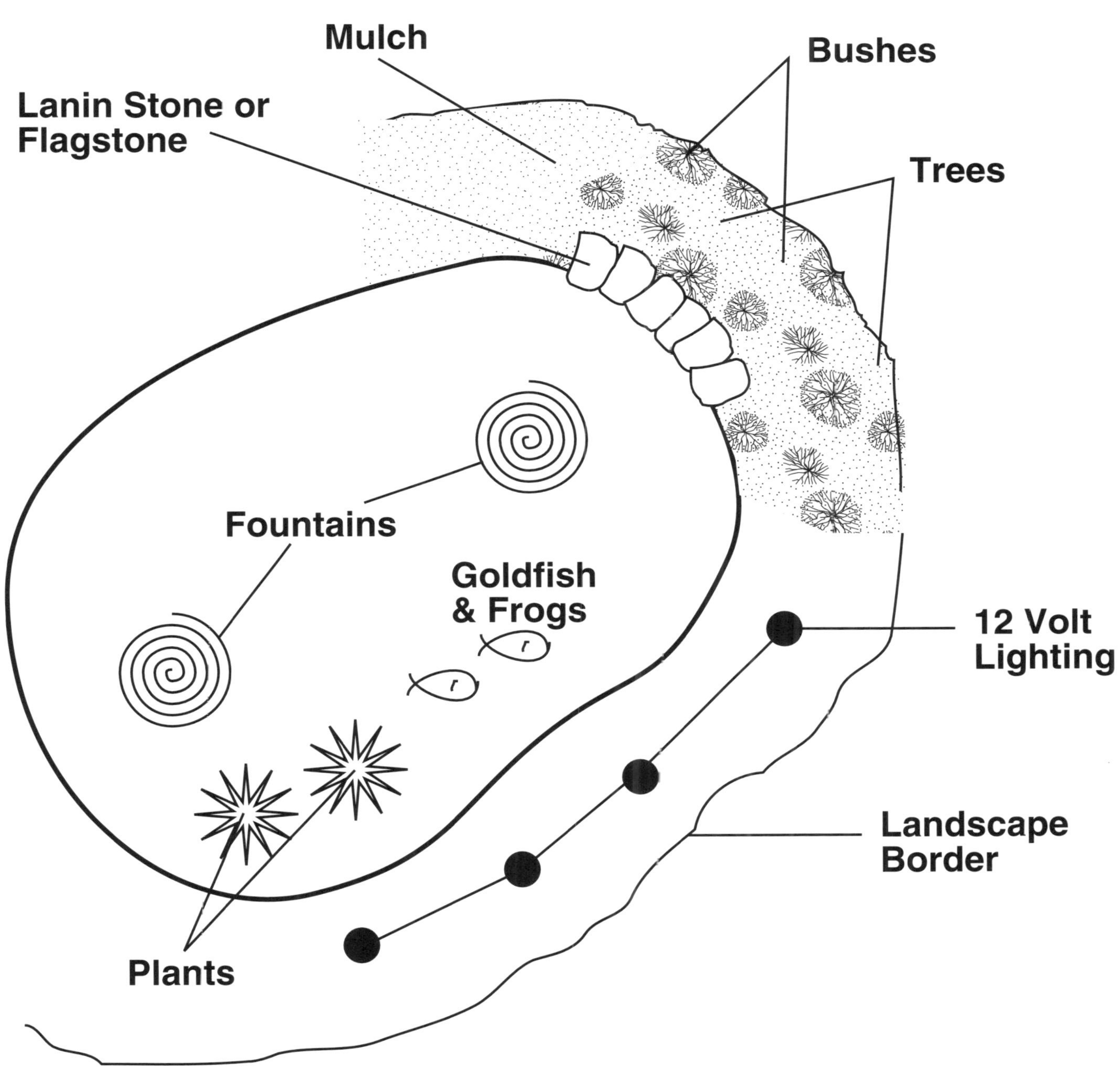
Mulch
Bushes
Lanin Stone or
Flagstone
Trees
Fountains
Goldfish
& Frogs
12 Volt
Lighting
Landscape
Border
Plants

POND FUNCTION/DESIGN

Ponds are similar to swimming pools. You have a water supply that should be filtered, chemically treated and maintained. Pond chemicals are readily available at most stores. Pond fish require special food that is found at aquatic life stores. A very small pump and cartridge filter will adequately keep the water clear and supply oxygen needed for fish. There are a number of fish species you can place in your pond. You can check with the local pet store to look into pond fish species. A well filtered pond can support and maintain aquatic life indefinitely. Your pond then becomes a large aquarium. Frogs, turtles and other aquatic life may find suitable living conditions within the pond.

Many different varieties of plant life are available to create an ecosystem. Underwater plants are inexpensive in bulb form. You can purchase them at most tropical fish stores. Plants are attractive and will enhance any setting.

The pond should be kept clean by using a skimmer net and a pool brush. Maintaining a pond is easy and required once a week. If you choose a small filtering system, the water will remain crystal clear. Add pond chemicals and maintain as needed. You would be surprised how large pond fish can grow. The basic pond mentioned in this guide contains a lot of water for potential ecosystem growth.

Pond lights can greatly enhance the setting. Twelve volt lighting systems are normally installed. These can be purchased at most stores. An array of colors are available. Simply position lights in the landscaping area near the pond. You may want to install a convenience electrical outlet for pond pumps, fountains and lights. A convenient water spigot may be added as well. A small pool light may be installed in the pond itself. Twelve volt pool lights can be set as the pond concrete base is poured. For an added bonus install a 1/2 inch pipe before pouring the pond base. Then attach a small air blower to the pipe outside the pond for a bubbling effect. Bubblers support aquatic life and add a functional dimension to the layout. Pipes may be installed prior to pond installation to connect to a small filter and pump. You can also use a plastic drain on the pond bottom to remove old unwanted water:

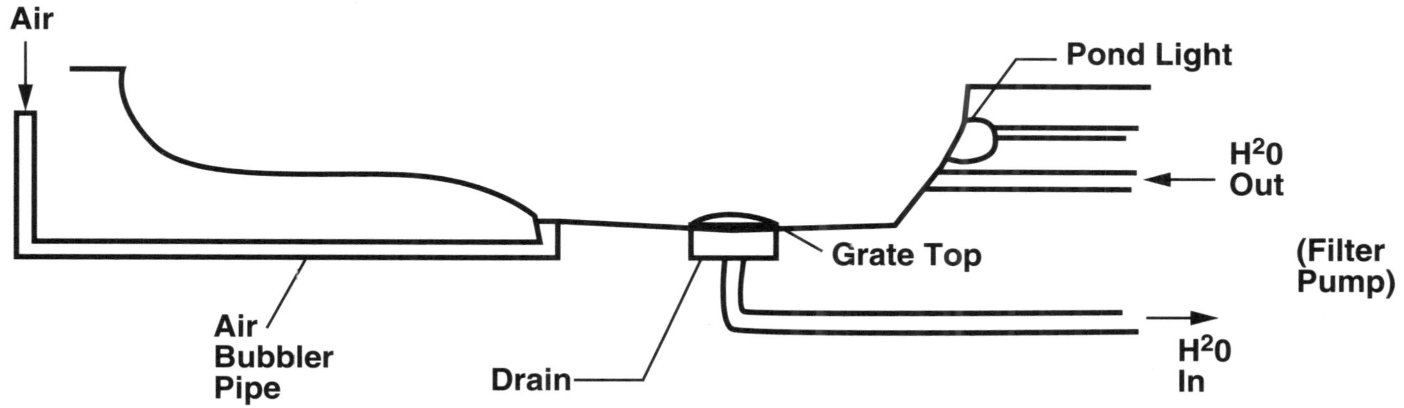

A waterfall is easily installed when the inlet line is positioned over stationary stone.

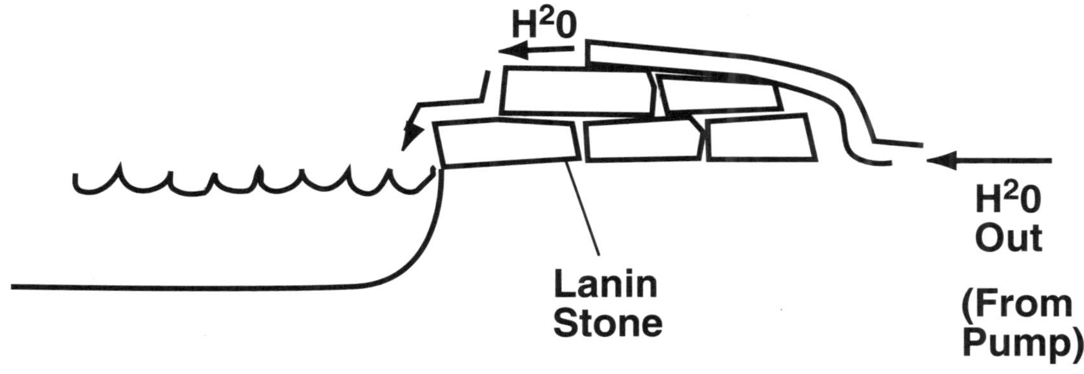

Large pond fish may be exciting to watch during feeding. A large number of fish may be placed because of the water capacity (one per gallon). At any rate aquatic life is interesting and easily cared for.

The cartridge filter must be removed and cleaned every 3-4 weeks. Simply remove the filter and spray with a garden hose. When the filter becomes difficult to clean you should purchase a new one. Small cartridge filters are inexpensive. A pressure gauge is usually installed at the cartridge filter, or you can install a tee in the inlet (H2O out line) and install a pressure gauge. Look to the filter manual for normal operating pressure. When the pressure is high, the filter requires cleaning; (read the instruction manual).

Pond pumps are normally 1/8-1/4 horsepower. They draw roughly 3.0 amps. Be sure to install a 24 hour automatic timer. Running times are normally (3-6) hours per day. A timer reduces maintenance and improves economy and pond performance. You can operate the pump after midnight to save money on electricity. The pump should have a lint pot basket to protect the impeller from larger debris. If not, then install a lint pot at the H2O intake line; a small screen may work. Ponds are fun to work with. In no time you will be able to easily maintain and care for the water.

Do not over feed the pond fish. Excess food can turn into bacteria and algae growth. Under feeding is smarter and the fish will appreciate the food more. If you have to enter the pond be careful. The concrete painted surface becomes very slippery.

Ponds are usually painted black with pool epoxy paint. Other colors are available and readily used: white, blue, green etc.. The painted surface can be made rather rough when common sand is added to the paint. Algae can create a very slippery surface.

As the drawing shows, a water fall can be added. The inlet line is positioned over stationary stone. This can add and enhance beauty and decorate the setting. The stationary stone or bricks should be permanently installed with brick mortar. Mortar is also used to seal the cracks and prevent leakage.

Another way to enhance the setting is to position the inlet to shoot water above the pond surface. This will add a lot of oxygen to the water supply, creating a splashing effect:

Decorative stone is usually flagstone or lanin stone. Lanin is somewhat expensive and flagstone may be used to reduce the cost. You may want to add a connecting sidewalk to the pond area. Purchase sidewalk decorative molds and mix concrete to install. This adds a nice touch to the surrounding area. A small patio is advisable and regular patio blocks can be positioned on sand. Simply excavate the ground area and install black plastic to control weed growth. Then add 2-3 inches of sand, and set patio blocks. They are available in different colors; black, white, blue, green etc..

POND FUNCTION/DESIGN

Sidewalk molds are of different shapes:

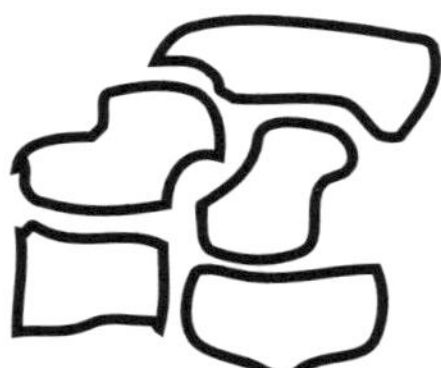

This is a popular sidewalk mold. A freeform design is easily installed. The ground should be excavated and sand base laid. Pour the mold, one section at a time. Gazebos are a nice added feature. They can be added later. Basic design:

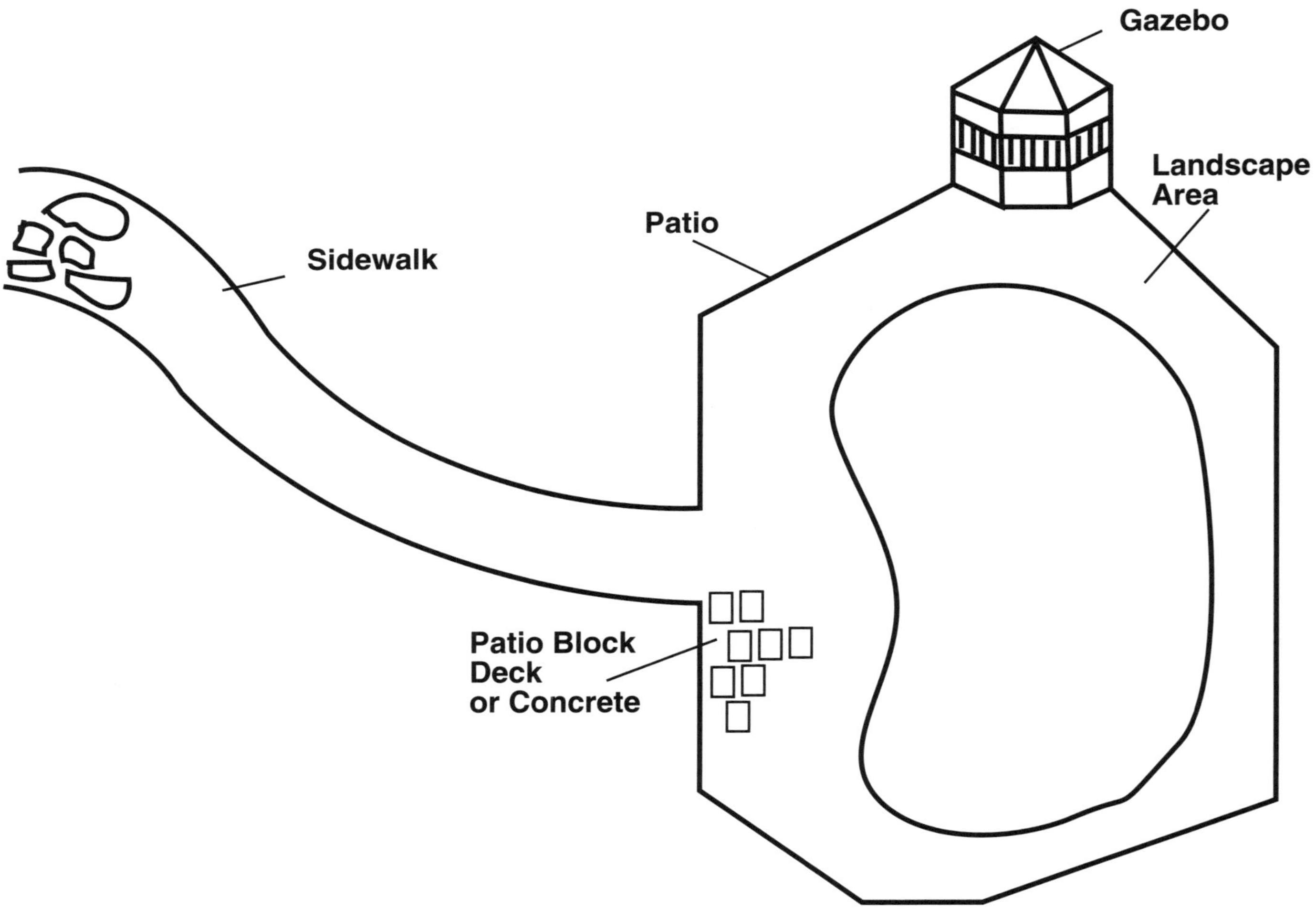

Gazebo

Landscape Area

Patio

Sidewalk

Patio Block
Deck
or Concrete

Pond decks can be concrete, patio blocks, Italian slate, flagstone, lanin stone, etc.. Black patio blocks staggered at 45 degrees are attractive. Concrete can be formed and poured 3-4 inches thick. Consider perfectly cut landscape timbers, inserted into the ground. It requires a little more work and expense, but very nice. Apply water seal to the deck to repel water. Here are just a few ideas to complete the perfect pond setting.

Gazebos can be constructed from many types of wood: cedar, pine, greenwood, etc.. Pre-made gazebos are available and can be purchased at many stores. Benches can be added, along with statues, rocks, etc.. As you can see, pond options can really enhance your natural background setting.

Landscape areas are discussed in the pond construction section. Again use your creativity to position bushes, trees and flowers. Mulch or stone can be installed in the landscape area. Mulch needs replacing periodically and regular 3/4 inch wash stone is sometimes preferred. Berms can be positioned outside the pond area. Berms are discussed in the new pool construction section. The earth removed from the pond can be utilized for landscaping, berms etc.. Landscaped berms add a new dimension to pond settings. Bushes, trees, flowers etc. can be added to the berm area.

Ponds may overflow with the addition of rain water. Be sure to under fill the water supply to allow for rain. Heavy rains will disturb normal pond water chemistry and chemicals should be added as needed. Water shield is available to reduce the growth of algae and weeds. I'm sure you have seen green tinted ponds. Water coloring will enhance the setting. Regular maintenance may require the removal of some water (1/4-1/2 of capacity) to flush the pond with fresh water. Flushing is an easy cleaning method to reduce maintenance. Another addition to the setting would be a smaller pond. You can connect the two water supplies together to act as one. A concrete runway joining the two will increase the amount of aquatic living space.

POND FUNCTION/DESIGN

A small wooden bridge may be constructed to improve the area. Join the bridge with a walkway and extend the lighting system near the bridge. Add the appropriate landscaping and it becomes a great concept. Bridges, gazebos, ponds, decking and landscaping make a wonderful area for out-door enjoyment. Add patio tables, chairs, barbecue grill and the area becomes a social area. The design work sheets included can greatly help you to plan and design an enjoyable pond area.

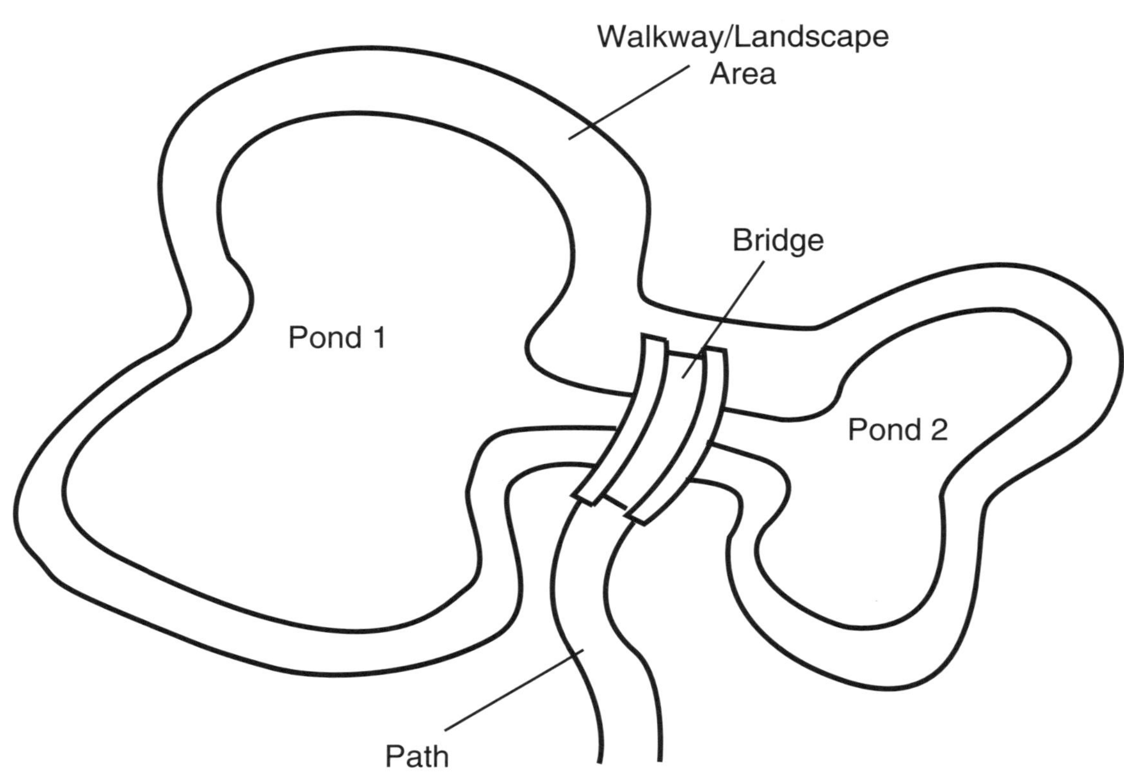

A two pond system may be a bit too much. The single pond is fun, functional, and will add beauty to your backyard. Fountains are frequently purchased for ponds. Again, a convenient electrical outlet would be great for functional items. The fountains may be connected to a timer. In fact, lighting, pumps and blowers can be timed as well. Timing pond components will decrease maintenance and pinpoint exact operating hours.

Lily pads are a nice addition to ponds. You can purchase lilies and other exotic plants at most stores. Proper plant conditions are important and proper information is needed. A fully functional , well planned and designed pond area can last and be enjoyed for years to come.

Poured concrete is a durable long lasting material that will last for 10 years plus if properly installed. Plastic ponds may fracture due to extreme temperature differences. Concrete is a functional, permanent material which has a relatively low cost. Anyone can pour a concrete pond with minimal finishing experience. Grade pins can pinpoint exact concrete grade at key locations.

The concrete grade will follow your intended curvature guide-pins. A rough finish is fine if a very smooth surface cannot be installed. The best way to install a pond is to find the outside perimeter. Use wood flexible forms and level as needed. Leveling forms should be accomplished with a transit. Upon leveling, the pond can be hand excavated or gravel raked to attain the desired grade. Many homeowners excavate the pond area then insert a plastic lining. You may be discouraged because plastic just isn't durable enough.

A good way to decide on a pond is to design and plan the area. Use the design worksheets and develop a workable site plan.

POND WORKSHEET

Pond ____________________

Pond Size: ____________________

Pool Shape: ____________________

Color: Black Blue White

Stone: Lanin Flag

Landscaping: Mulch Washstone

Bushes: ____________________

Trees: ____________________

Filtering system: ____________________

Lights: ____________________

Fountains: ____________________

Air bubbler: ____________________

Drain: ____________________

Waterfall: ____________________

Fish: ____________________

Aquatic life: ____________________

Plants: ____________________

NOTES

NOTES

Wall panels for liner pools are usually steel (G-235 rated), or structural foam. Any inground pool kit purchased should include pool specification sheets. These sheets locate wall panel positions and should be followed as shown. I have included some specification sheets which show construction methodology, structural details and longitudinal sections. These pool plans are actually pre-approved for liner pool construction. These sheets can be submitted, along with specifications and dimension sheets to Building and Zoning for building permits.

Panel layout is routine: skimmers are located on the house side, while inlets are positioned on the opposite side. Walls are bolted together with fasteners provided. Be sure to perfectly flush panels. The walls must be squared, leveled and installed with braces. Once the walls are positioned, rebar is driven into the walls for the concrete footing.

Steel walls are extremely strong and ductile. Once a 6-12 inch footing is poured, the structure can support a small home. The steel is zinc-coated (G-235 rated), rust protected. G-235 walls are strong, and will last for years. Most manufactures warranty these panels for up to 30 years. A continuous constant concrete footing strengthens the steel structure and is unsurpassed. The footing and wall act as one.

Structural foam is currently being used for walls, featuring high tensile parallel and perpendicular strength. The real advantage is water/chemical resistance. Foam walls are lightweight and easier to install. Early foam walls had a few problems but newer foam has been improved for strength and longevity. Again a 6-12 inch concrete footing is poured and the wall and footing act as one.

Aluminum walls are seldom used because of the higher costs. The panels must be made considerably thicker to achieve the proper strength.

Once a wall panel is selected the installation is next. Lay out panels according to pool specification sheets, bolt together, square and level. Install adjustable braces and insert rebar as needed. Take your time and install the wall panels properly. Panel placement is both fun and rewarding. If you have contracted the installation, this information will help you to understand wall panel placement.

Once the walls are completely assembled, and if you have purchased 4 X 8 ft rovel stairs, they are inserted into the end or side. Use the pool specification sheets to properly install. Usually, drilling holes is necessary to attach the stair to the pool. Align the concrete receiver to the stair top level, and flush the stair edge to the wall panels. Drill holes and install bolts. Most stairs have steel supporters attached to the stair bottom. Simply detach supporters and install under stair. Add braces to stairs as needed.

Panels can be adjusted manually to align the top edge. Simply tighten or loosen as needed. Now you have the wall panels set and secured.
A concrete footing is poured, and the walls are permanently installed.
A trick to insure proper level is to check the pool grade height after the footing is poured. Raise or lower the walls while the concrete is wet. It is a good idea to pour the control slab near the house after the footing. Simply form a concrete slab 4 X 8 ft.. Excavate ground 8 inches below the concrete for gravel and pour 4 inches of concrete. Install a small piece of wire mesh and grade the gravel constant. Once the walls are set, the remaining work is accomplished. As I mentioned before an experienced wall-setter knows a lot of tricks to perfect installation. Be sure the panels are set perfectly before attempting to pour the concrete footing.

Vermiculite/Portland mixture is commonly used for pool base material. The materials are placed into a cement mixer and troweled to finish on the pool bottom. Water is added in the mixer and a hard bottom is obtained.
Vermiculite is the best and most expensive pool base used in the industry.
A soft abrasive, hard bottom that will not damage the liner upon fracturing.
Vermiculite is like super glue that is self-supporting. The material adheres to steel amazingly well! A lightweight material used to hold water in soil.
Different grades of vermiculite are available: #1, #2, #3, etc.. #2 is normally used, and can be purchased at garden shops.

Vermiculite is somewhat difficult to work with, and must be poured at a constant thickness. The mixer is loaded with water, portland, and vermiculite and mixed together until a consistency is obtained.

Sand/cement is another pool base that is frequently used. Again a cement mixer combines the materials together to a desired consistency.
Sand/cement is a less expensive compound compared to vermiculite.
Vermiculite is very lightweight. Sand/cement is heavy and a lot more work to install. Regular sand is sometimes installed, but not recommended.
Above ground pool bases are fine mason sand, wetted and troweled to finish. A sand bottom could be ruined in 4-5 years. Never use sand as a pool base when building an inground pool.

After the pool base is poured, wall foam is installed. Foam insulates and protects the wall from the liner. A concrete finish edge is installed to receive the liner beading. White aluminum is normally used, and will last for many years. The pool is now ready for the lining.

Vinyl liners are made to perfectly fit a measured dimension area. Be sure the liner specifications are correct. Depend on a professional pool builder to install it properly. The liner is installed with a vacuum/blower by removing the air from between the liner and wall. At this time the pool is filled with water.

Your house supply water should be adequate. Hauled in water can be very expensive. The best way to save money is to fill with your garden hose. Two days are required to completely fill most pools. If a well is being used, be sure to turn the water off when the house supply water is in use. Another safeguard is to give the well pump a rest after filling the pool four hours. If you have iron problems, corrective steps must be taken to clean the liner. The best way to clean a pool filled with iron is to let the debris settle, then vacuum with the pool pump.

For convenience locate a water spigot near the pool deck. Simply attach a hose valve at your existing water spigot, run .75 inch poly pipe to a landscaper's timber, install a new spigot on the timber. Water can be used for deck cleaning, pool filling, etc.. A water line can be installed from inside the house to the new spigot near the pool. (A licensed plumber would be required). Auto-filling devices are also available. These also must be plumbed from the house. Auto-filling devices may have problems, and are difficult to replace. As explained, liner pools are very popular and widely used in many areas of the U.S.. They are inexpensive and maintenance-free.

A liner pool can last for many years with little or no repair. The installation process must be completed perfectly. The major advantage is the pool's resilience to extreme weather changes. Liner pools are installed in the north and the south as well. Many homeowners choose liner pools for economy, longevity and improved pool performance.

LINER POOL PLANS

Building/Zoning departments require plans. These are submitted to subdivision committees, Health departments, subcontractors and workers. I have included some basic detailed drawings. These plans have been submitted to many midwestern zoning agencies. They display the best methodology available and are pre-approved. The actual pool dimensions, bonding and electrical details should be included. Normally you must obtain a land plot plan and draw the location of your inground swimming pool. Check with various local agencies for the requirements in your area. Underground water systems must be referenced and located; septic systems, wells, drainage tiles, sewer, etc..

These plans are a useful tool to familiarize and provide an overview of basic liner pool construction. Most home owners hire a swimming pool construction company to do the actual building. Because builders know all the tricks of pool construction, they should be hired for their services. Swimming pool construction is extremely difficult and no expense should be spared to attain the desired results.

This guide and these plans will be of great help to anyone interested in buying a new inground pool. Dealers spend countless hours educating home owners about pools and accessories. The basic idea is to read the guide carefully and gain the necessary knowledge to buy the right pool for you and your family.

CONCRETE DECK DETAIL

Pitch = 1/4" per ft.

Scale = 1/2" per ft.

Concrete: 6 Bag Mix

Thickness: 4"

STRUCTURAL DETAIL

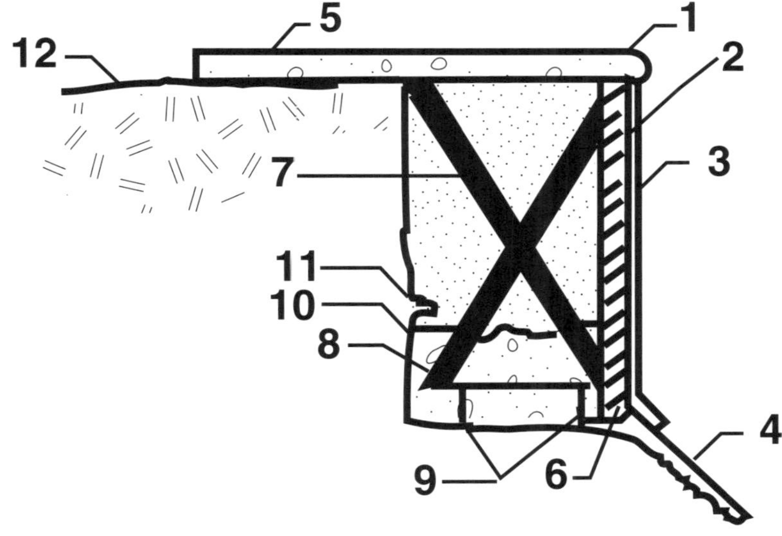

1. Aluminum Extrusion
2. Wall Foam
3. 20 Mil Vinyl Liner
4. Vermiculite Cement Mixture 2-3" thick
5. Concrete Deck
6. Steel Wall- 14 gauge -G-235 Zinc Coated
7. Concrete Deck Support System- 14 gauge Steel
8. A-Frame Brace-10 gauge Steel-/Zinc
9. Rebar-1/2" Ø
10. Concrete footing-6-12" - (5 Bag Mix)
11. Pea Gravel
12. Undisturbed Earth

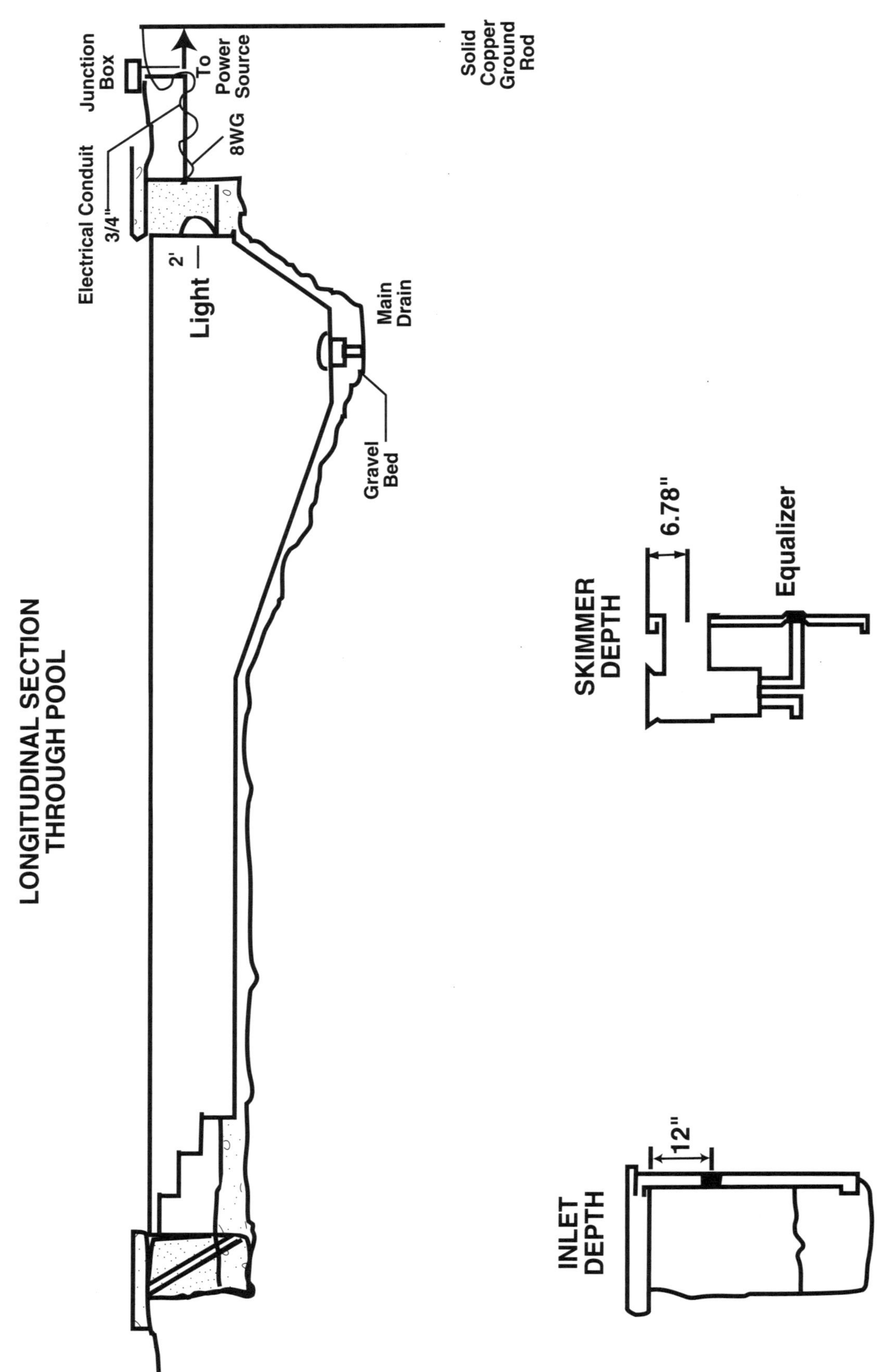
Junction Box
To Power Source
Solid Copper Ground Rod
Electrical Conduit
3/4"
8WG
2'
Light
Main Drain
Gravel Bed
LONGITUDINAL SECTION THROUGH POOL
SKIMMER DEPTH
6.78"
Equalizer
INLET DEPTH
12"

Water for swimming pools should be clean and iron-sulfur free. Well water usually contains iron and special care must be taken.

Many people have swimming pool water hauled in. This water is usually very clean, but the cost can be prohibitive. City water is great for swimming pools.

If you have well supply water, simply clean and shock the pool. Most well water is somewhat clean and inexpensive. You can save a lot of money by using your well. Be sure not to use additional water for clothes, showers, etc..

A good way to use a well is to fill the pool in four hour periods, giving the system a 1/2 hour break between periods.

Using clean crystal clear water will help to eliminate any initial maintenance. Any additional water should be added to the pool skimmer to be filtered and chemically treated.

Pool water spigots can be installed near the pool for easy access. Simply install a landscape timber (in concrete) and a spigot from your house supply or extend the water supply from an existing outside water outlet.
An extended water supply will provide easy access for pool cleaning and additional water needed for the pool.

Pool water can be automatically added with a special device, usually plumbed from your home. A separate water outlet can also be installed in the pool wall and water added as needed.

Anti-siphon fittings should be installed on existing spigots for pool water. Many municipalities require anti-siphon devices.
At any rate, additional spigots located near the pool make it convenient to clean the deck and add water.

CHEMICALS/MAINTENANCE TIPS

Maintaining an inground pool should be fun and easy. Here are a few tips that will improve swimming pool performance and decrease maintenance by as much as 80%. Implement these ideas to provide a carefree pool.

INSTALL:

1. **Automatic switch for pump/filter (24 hr., 115 volt)**
2. **Off-line Chlorinator**
3. **Automatic cleaner**
4. **Solar reel/cover**

An automatic switch (24 hr. timer) will operate the pump/filter a specified period of time, eliminating over/under filtering. The timer should be set to automatically operate the pump/filter to provide efficiency and performance during the early morning hours. The best time to run the pump is between 12-6 AM. when the electric rates are lower.

Automatic chlorination and night filtering will prepare the pool for each new swimming day. A chlorinator will improve water balance and provide crystal clear pool water all summer long.

Chlorinators distribute a constant supply of chemicals to the pool by injecting chlorine into the total water supply. Extra inlets are crucial for even distribution. An off-line system is better because it by-passes the filter, pump and heater to eliminate corrosive chemical damage to components. The chlorine canister capacity is 8 lbs. of 1 inch tablets, lasting up to 4 weeks. The chlorinator mounts to the control center, and is easily assembled and installed.

Installing an auto-cleaner will maintain a clean bottom and sides. There are two types.

1. **Inlet connection cleaners**
2. **Skimmer suction cleaners**

Inlet cleaners normally operate with an independent booster pump. The pump must be connected at the filter/pump. For this system, a separate inlet should be installed at the time of pool construction. Robot cleaners traverse along bottom and sides, pushing water downward and forcing dirt, debris and leaves into a net. The net must be cleaned periodically. The robot cleaner is preferred over all cleaners, and is fun to watch. Other inlet cleaners work similarly, pushing water into a net to collect debris, cleaning the pool bottom.

Skimmer suction cleaners plug into the existing skimmer and operate from the pool pump. They require no booster pump so they perform efficiently and effectively. These cleaners work slowly, vacuuming the entire pool. Skimmer cleaners are inexpensive and popular. Automatic cleaners operating during the early morning hours (12-6 AM) will prepare your pool for each new day of swimming. Simply remove the cleaner before pool usage.

Solar reel/cover systems allow you to easily install/remove the solar cover. Solar covers decrease heat and chemical dissipation, trapping ultraviolet rays under the pool surface providing heat to the pool water.

Reel systems are positioned on the pool end, near the diving board. You can easily reel the cover on the tube. Reel systems are inexpensive and require some assembly.

Vacuum, brush and skim the pool periodically. Leaves and debris must be removed. A fully automatic pool cleaning system should eliminate most manual cleaning.

Check skimmer and empty pump baskets periodically. Leaves and debris can clog the filtering system rapidly.

Pool Chemicals

Some pool chemicals can be expensive and troublesome. Chlorine is an inexpensive water treatment which is available in tablet form. One inch tablets are used in auto-chlorinators to continuously feed water with fresh chlorine. Buy large quantities (50-100 lbs) to save money. This supply should last 2-3 years, depending upon the pool size and summer weather conditions. Stabilizers are sometimes used to reduce chlorine consumption. Stabilizers are expensive and their use to save on chlorine is not always cost effective.

Liquid chlorine should always be on hand to burn out algae and to add additional chlorine during hot summer days when the pool might be overused. Add 2-3 gallons and be sure to run the pump to evenly mix and distribute into the total water supply. Shock the pool water when opening and closing and during the summer months.

Algaecide must be used to prevent algae growth. Algae easily slides off liner pools and is difficult to remove from concrete, marcite or fiberglass. The best way to remove algae is to shock the pool with 5-10 gallons of chlorine, then vacuum and clean pool sides and bottom. Don't waste money on expensive algaecides to remove algae: instead, add shock. Algaecide should be bought in case lots to save money. One case is equal to 12 quarts. That should last up to two years. Preventing algae growth is the key to simplifying pool care.

Cloudy Pool Water

If the pool turns cloudy, use your test kit to check chlorine and PH level. When chlorine level is low shock the pool with 5 gallons of liquid chlorine, then run the filter/pump until water clears.

If the chlorine and PH level are too high, then add 1-2 gallons of muriatic acid. Operate pump/filter to distribute muriatic acid 1-2 days and your pool will clear.

Be sure to backwash the filter or clean your filter cartridge system when the pool water clouds. Improper filtering will cause cloudy water as well.

Balancing your pool water is important and not difficult. Target chlorine concentration to 1.0 part per million, the ideal range on the test kit. When chlorine is in the ideal range (1.0 ppm.), then check the PH level. The ideal range is 7.2-7.6, the exact PH of the liquid in your eyes. Use PH (minus) or (plus) to adjust the PH level.

Crystal clear, clean pool water is a product of proper filtering and the addition of correct chemicals. Be sure to read the section on functions, filtering and heating. A powerful pump (1.0-1.5 HP.) will maintain a cleaner pool. An adequate sand filter is also needed, along with the installation of fresh clean sand every year. Operate the pool filtering system and add chemicals at night, automatically. 12-6 AM is the best time to filter and add chemicals. Crystal clear water is easily attained with planning and problem solving methods.

CHECK LIST

AUTOMATIC 24 HR. TIMER ____YES ____NO

OFF-LINE CHLORINATOR ____YES ____NO

AUTOMATIC CLEANER ____YES ____NO

SOLAR POOL/COVER ____YES ____NO

POOL CHEMICALS____

____

____

FILTER:		SAND		EARTH		CARTRIDGE
PUMP (H.P.):		.75		1.0		1.5
HEATER SIZE:	125,000	150,000	175,000	200,000	250,000	300,000

VACUUM KIT: ____YES ____NO

TYPE: ____CLEAR WEIGHTED ____NON WEIGHTED

BRUSH ____YES ____NO

WATER READINGS

To improve pool water conditions and solve water problems

	Chlorine	P.H.	Temp./cond.
EXAMPLE:	1.0 ppm.	7.8	75°/sunny
Sunday	__________	__________	__________
Monday	__________	__________	__________
Tuesday	__________	__________	__________
Wednesday	__________	__________	__________
Thursday	__________	__________	__________
Friday	__________	__________	__________
Saturday	__________	__________	__________

Vacuum Procedure

Assemble vacuum head, handle and hose, insert into pool. Fill vacuum hose with water to displace air: (use pool inlets or hose).
Select the filter position on the multi-port valve, turn the pump on, close the main drain valve and operate one skimmer; (single vacuum line suction).
Connect the vacuum hose to the vacuum suction plate and insert it into the skimmer.
Check water flow at the inlets and allow the pump to prime with water.
Vacuum the entire pool, and backwash as needed.

Filter backwashing

Refer to the Filter/Heater section.

Select **BACKWASH** position on the multi-port valve. Turn pump on and view the site glass.
When water turns clear, turn pump off and select the **RINSE** position.
Turn pump on and view the site glass again. When water turns clear, shut pump off, and select **FILTER**. Backwash after vacuuming and periodically (once per week).
Backwash when your filter pressure is 20-25 psi.

FILTERING/PUMP LEAKS

Leaks are common at the filter/pump. There are many seals that must be replaced periodically. Be sure to correct O-ring seal leaks.

A common leak is at the pump housing: after the water is accelerated from the impeller, the water pressure is great and will cause a leak at the pump housing female thread connector. The male connection should be resealed every year with neoprene sealer.

Pump leaks must be eliminated to ensure proper filter performance. Replumbing the filter/pump and heater is common. Check the rubber seals at the pump and filter: replace as needed. Obtain a filter/pump diagram to locate all seals and replace as needed.

Underground plumbing leak prevention is discussed in the winterizing section. Plumbing leaks are the main cause of improper filtering and must be corrected. To locate underground leaks, lower the pool water level below the inlets. If the pool doesn't leak, the problem is in the underground plumbing.

(Planned method to improve pool care)

DATE:

__________ Sunday: ____

____

____

__________ Monday: ____

____

____

__________ Tuesday: ____

____

____

__________ Wednesday: ____

____

____

__________ Thursday: ____

____

____

__________ Friday: ____

____

____

__________ Saturday: ____

____

____

SPRING POOL OPENINGS

The best time to open the inground pool is in early spring. The water is usually very cold and crystal clear. Ice thaws in late march, and spring begins in April.

Pump operation
You don't need to operate the filter pump in April. You can open the pool early and wait until the season begins to filter/heat the water. Chlorine concentration does not dissipate in colder weather.

Covers
First, remove water from the winter cover surface, then pull the cover from the pool. Be sure to lay the cover out and clean with a disinfectant. Covers should be stored in a cool, dry place to prevent dry rot. Vinyl and solid poly covers must be cleaned and stored. Stretch poly mesh covers never need cleaning.

Purchase a pump cover and fishing net. Pump water from cover and remove leaves with the net. It will be necessary to prepare the pool for the opening, so at pre-pool opening remove water and leaves.

Filter Pump
If you have read the section on winterizing, the filter, pump motor and heater must be reinstalled. Start with the filter tank. Pour in fresh silica sand. Install pump motor, usually four bolts mounted to the pump lint pot. Check rubber seals, lubricate and tighten bolts.

Heater
Place the pool heater in position and connect inlet/outlet water connections. Tighten the gas line coupling and turn valve on. Use a manual igniter to light the pilot assembly. Next turn the heater on, position at comfort zone, to test heater with the filter/pump running.

RV, Extensions, Tube
Remove the blow out extensions, or plugs, to operate the filter/pump, circulating pool water, and removing RV antifreeze. RV will mix into your water supply. Water tubes should be emptied, cleaned and stored. Expansion pillows, and or Plastic Barrows must be removed, cleaned, and stored.

Pool Cleaning
Vacuum pool bottom, brush and clean sides. Clean pool as needed. Add 5-10 gallons of liquid chlorine. Operate pump filter 24-30 hrs.

Flushing

Improper winterizing can cause dirty black water. The best thing to do is flush the pool with fresh water, or remove all of the tainted water. Simply remove water and refill with your house supply.

Tainted water is usually discarded. Empty the pool and refill with fresh tap water. You can spend a lot of money on chemicals and filtering to clean tainted water.

Tainted water can severely stain the pool bottom, and sides. If your pool has a liner, liquid chlorine can remove staining. Concrete/marcite bottoms must be shocked with caution to prevent deterioration from strong chemical oxidation. Many concrete/gunite pools are emptied, then muriatic acid is applied and pool is refilled. Have this done professionally. Muriatic acid fumes are dangerous.

Your pool water should be crystal clear in spring; if not, the following are a few remedies.

POTENTIAL PROBLEMS:

1. **Pool deck pitched improperly**
2. **Pool not cleaned properly at closing**
3. **Water not shocked properly**
4. **Winter cover torn**
5. **Winter cover fell into pool**
6. **Melting snow and rain inadvertently drained into pool**

The pool decking should be pitched 1/4 inch per foot away from the pool; otherwise rain and melting snow will pour into the pool and cause water to turn green and black. Usually a drain tile must be installed behind the pool deck to reroute excess water to other property areas. Drain tiles are discussed in the new pool construction section. When constructing a new inground pool, be sure a proper pitch is provided to prevent later problems.

If the deck is improperly pitched, you must install a seal barrier to prevent water from entering the pool. You can use water tubes, sand bags or plastic. Installing water tubes in a double row is an easy way to detour water. Sand bags work well. Plastic bars can be mounted to your pool deck with anchoring bolts.

SPRING POOL OPENINGS

Be sure to clean the pool perfectly when closing. Read the section on chemical/maintenance tips. Maintaining a clean pool will promote long life and less problems.

Refer to the winterizing section. With pool water crystal clear, shock pool with 5-10 gallons of liquid chlorine and mix evenly with pool filter/pump: 5 gallons for smaller pools (10-18,000 gallons). Shocking the pool will burn out bacteria and oxidize the water supply.(A low concentration of chlorine will remain in the water until the pool opening.) Reshock the pool in the spring. Proper shocking will maintain a clear pool and eliminate water problems in the spring.

Large trees could overload winter covers with leaves and branches, causing rips and tears, mixing tainted water into clear water. Covers should be repaired before being reused.

Pools near large trees should be carefully covered. A good method is to install a less expensive cover so replacement cost is lower. Installing an expensive cover which can be irreparably damaged by falling leaves and branches is not economical. Install the inexpensive cover and secure it with ropes, stakes and water tubes. The cover, tubes and ropes can easily be replaced. Cover damage is usually due to the accumulated branch and leaf weight. Early fall closing is usually necessary to avoid leaf and branch accumulation in the pool.

Proper cover securing is mandatory. Stability will provide a safe, durable and dependable pool-cover system. Covers that slip into the pool are usually allowed to remain there until Spring. Winter covers are discussed in the winterizing section. Follow the simplified methodology for closing. Careful selection and installation is the key to improved pool water maintenance. Inground pools that are properly winterized will increase their life expectancy and improve ongoing pool functions.

Poly stretch covers attach to solid brass anchors recessed in the pool decking. Simply expose anchors screws with an allen wrench. Stretch covers are properly supported with the anchors. Regular covers may slip into the pool water. Heavy rain or wind storms may cause a regular cover to detach from pool decking. Be sure to tie rope to cover eye hooks and secure to anchors or wood stakes into the ground.

When snow begins to melt and heavy rain accumulates, excess water may flow under the pool cover and mix with treated water. There are a few ways to eliminate excess water:

1. **Proper pool deck pitch**
2. **Drainage tiles installed behind the pool decking**

Improper pitch is discussed earlier in this section.

Drainage tiles are frequently installed behind the pool deck. The new pool construction section illustrates a typical tile installation. Tiles must be pitched and installed properly. Pitch should be 1/4 to 1/2 inch per foot. The best way to install tiles is to first excavate the drainage trench, pitch to a lower elevation and line the trench with heavy gauge plastic.

Pour in 2 inches of 3/4 inch wash stone and install the 3-4" diameter plastic tubing tile. Block off the ends and buy fittings to connect additional tile. Next, hold tubing into place and add stone to completely submerge tiles. You should always install tile to reroute rain, melting snow and pool splash water. Otherwise water will accumulate at the concrete-grade edge and cause soil saturation and erosion.

CURTAIN DRAIN

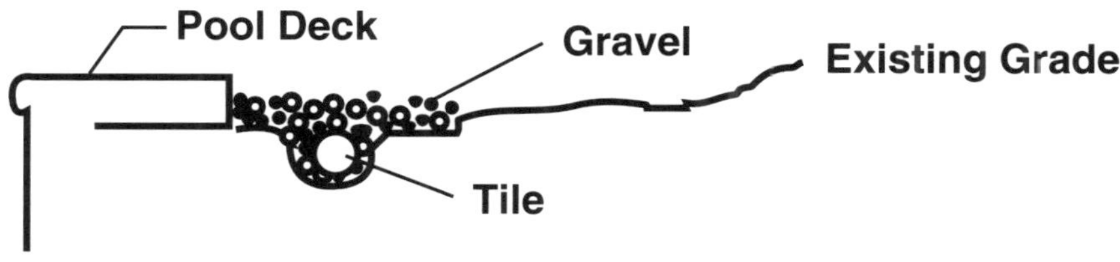

This is called a maximum guard protection (MGP) system. Excess water can seep under the deck near the pool wall, causing damage. Protecting your pool from water seepage is smart. You will also enjoy the look of gravel beyond the pool deck. Curtain drains can be accurately excavated with an 8"-12" wide trencher or by hand. The installation cost is inexpensive.

Curtain drains reduce concrete damage and extend pool and deck life. Tiles are always mandatory when your pool elevation is lower than the yard grade. A typical drain system will reroute large amounts of excess water every year:

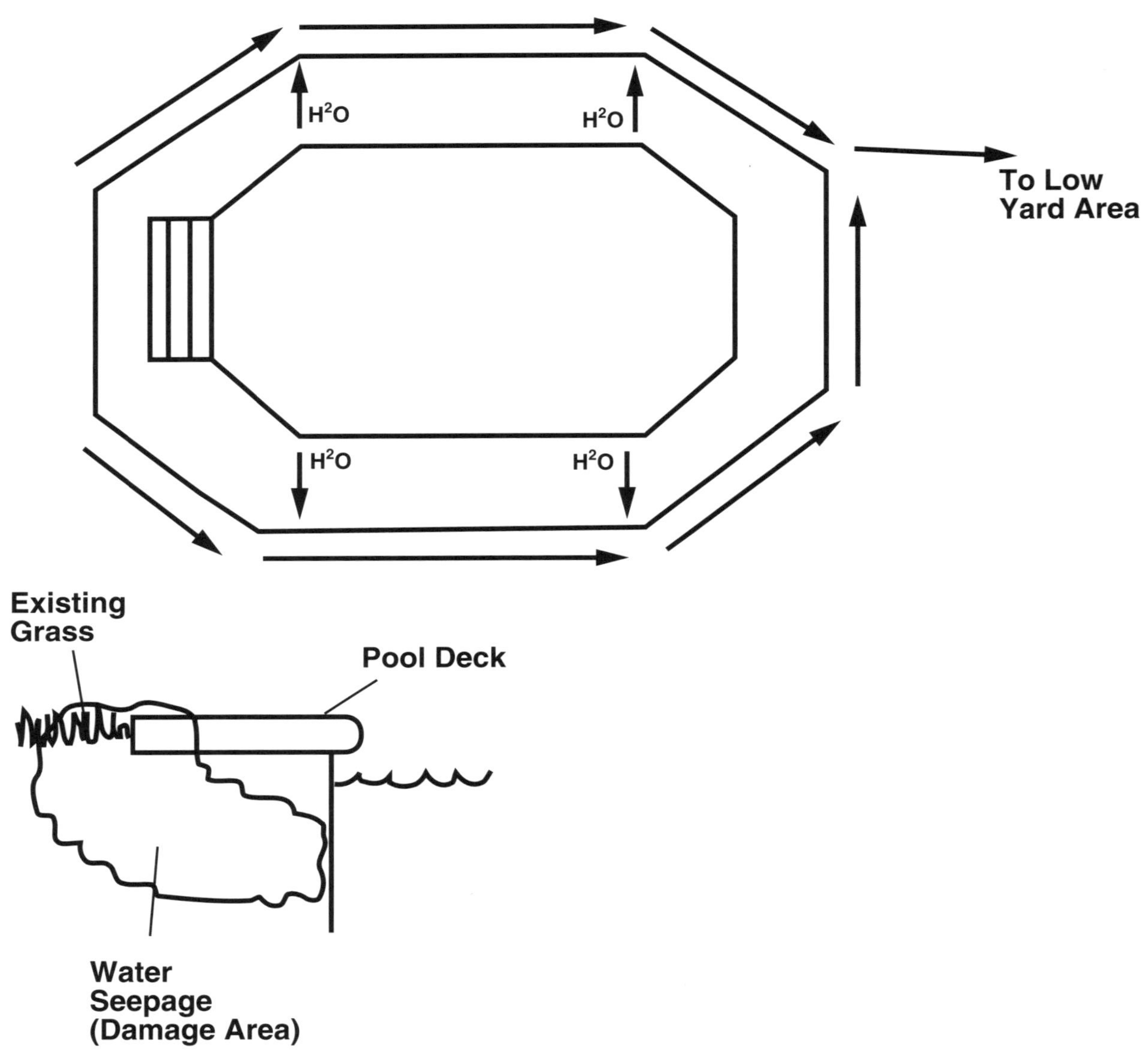

Water seepage causes soil erosion. After a few months underground holes will form, causing supported concrete to crack, reducing pool deck life. Tiles should always be installed to protect your pool, and eliminate excess water damage.

Winterizing an inground pool is extremely important. You can extend the life of your pool and equipment by properly winterizing. Caution must be taken to ensure continuing pool functions. If you winterize improperly, the consequences could be troublesome. Large repair bills are common. I will discuss the best possible method to protect your pool and equipment from severe winter conditions. We will list potential problems, then solve them by winterizing techniques.

Potential problem list:
Damage to:

1. **Underground Plumbing**
2. **Pool light conduit**
3. **Sand filter/pump motor**
4. **Heater**
5. **Pool Structure**

Underground plumbing is frequently fractured by sub-zero temperatures. You must be sure to winterize properly. First, remove all water from pipes by using a high-powered blower (2.5-3.0) HP.; then completely fill plumbing with anti-freeze. Removing water and RV installation is somewhat tricky. I have designed a method which will allow you to easily winterize the plumbing.

Plumbing is very important and is discussed in many previous sections. Proper winterizing will improve pool performance by eliminating potential fractures. Air leaks are common in plumbing and are caused by improper winterizing. This will adversely effect ongoing pool operations. Above ground plumbing should be air dried and filled with clean RV anti-freeze. Many pool owners experience air leaks and preventive action is required to prevent them. Air leaks will prevent proper pump priming and disrupt normal water flow. They are detected by viewing the inlet water flow and recognizing pressure fluctuations.

WINTERIZING Blowout Extensions

The best method is to use blowout extensions. Extensions are a fitted pvc pipe elbow, extending your inlets and skimmers above the existing plumbing and water level. This method allows you to remove all water easily and fill pipes with anti-freeze without any air gaps or voids. Most pipe fractures occur behind the pool wall, and installing extensions will ensure your protection in these problem areas.

Listen closely while you blow air and add anti-freeze. You can actually hear the pipes displacing air with RV. Extensions are a safety feature, allowing a slight pressure to maintain a constant level of anti-freeze, designed to safeguard your plumbing from fracture and freezing. Be sure to leave an air-gap for RV-expansion:

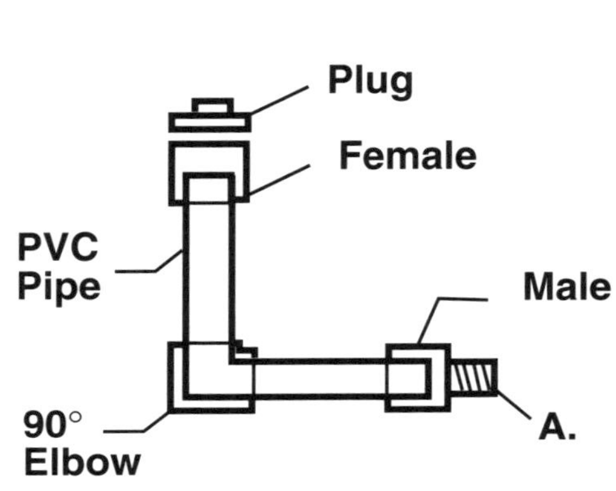

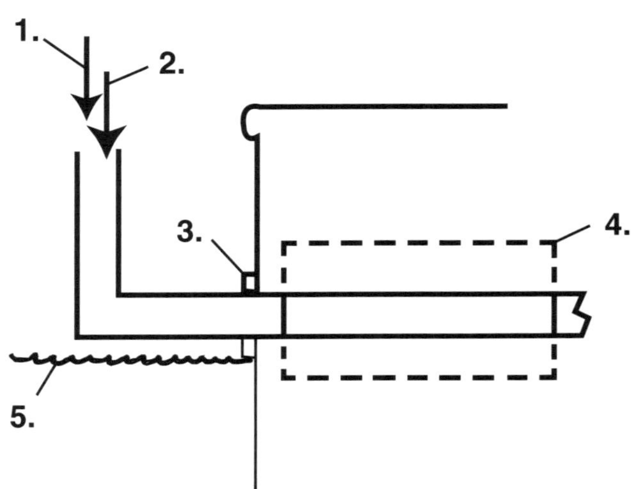

BLOWOUT EXTENSION DESIGN
(High pressure fittings)
(1.5 inch)
A. Apply Teflon tape and silicone

1. Blow Air
2. Fill with RV anti freeze
3. Inlets
4. Problem Area
5. Winter $H^2 0$ Level

AIR GAP

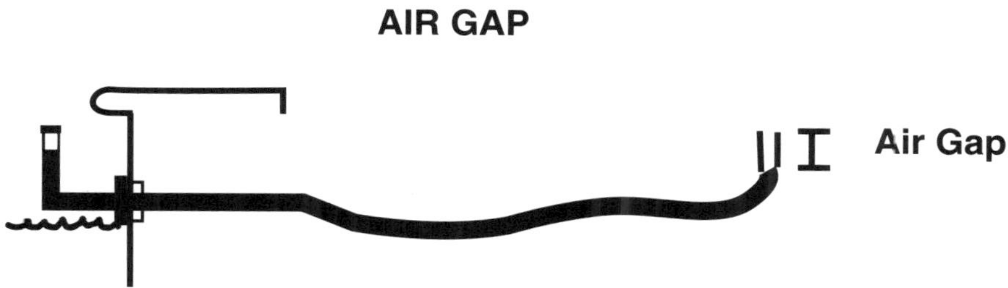

Note: When winterizing the main drain line, pour-in 2-3 gallons of RV anti-freeze, blow air into line and close valve, creating an air lock.
Your pool light should be removed, cord uncoiled, and placed on the concrete deck. Be sure to remove bulb and glass lens from the light assembly. When your light is installed, be sure to use a heavy wall plastic conduit to eliminate any fractures. Many electricians use lightweight PVC which will easily freeze and break, causing problems. If your light leaks, seal the conduit to the light assembly cord:

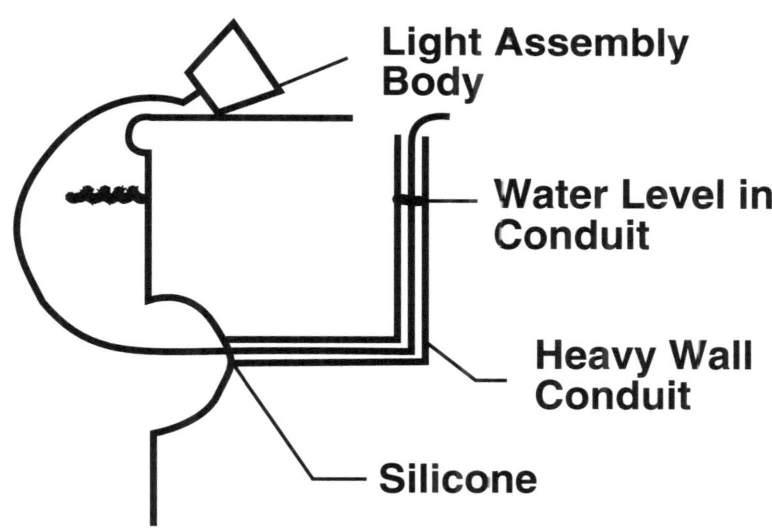

WINTERIZING Cold & Ice Damage

SAND FILTERS should be emptied of all sand, disconnected and stored in the winter months. You will avoid the sub-zero temperatures that will wear plastic parts and damage rubber seals. Your filter will last 10 years or more if you store it away: otherwise, winter weather will shorten the tank life. Purchase a split tank to easily remove/install filter sand. Fresh sand should be installed every year to maximize filter/pump performance.

PUMP MOTORS should also be disconnected and stored. They could freeze up in the winter months and may cause you expense in the spring. Pump impeller seals and plastic parts could crack and damage easily. Your pump will last for 6 years or longer if you disassemble and store.

HEATER EXCHANGER PIPE fracturing and cast iron damage is common in subzero temperatures. It is recommended you store heaters away from the cold to eliminate any winter damage. Be sure to remove all water. Air-dry water headers and heat exchanger to prevent rusting.

STRUCTURAL DAMAGE due to the winter months is rare for most in ground swimming pools; however, special care is taken to prevent ice thrust (ice expansion), especially when your pool has a fiberglass or structural foam wall. We prevent thrust by placing plastic barrows and expansion pillows in the pool water. Barrows and pillows disrupt expansion by not allowing the ice to freeze at a constant depth throughout the pool surface.

ICE THRUST

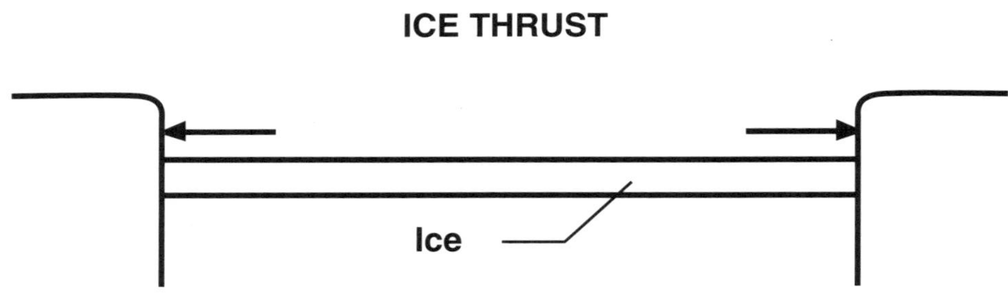

ICE THRUST PREVENTION

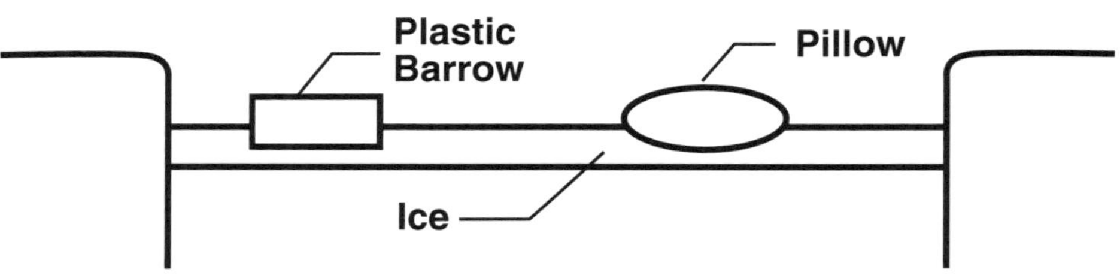

Prepping pool water before closing is important to ensure clear water in the spring. Be sure the pool is cleaned and water filtered. Shock pool, add algaecide and mix them into the total water supply. The pool will remain clear all winter long, due to decreasing chemical dissipation with the lower water temperature. If the pool deck is pitched properly, rain water and melting snow will flow away from pool. Be sure to close the pool in early fall, and open in early spring. By doing this, your water will remain clearer. If you wait until June, the water could be extremely dirty. Ladders/handrails are easily removed from their anchors. Polish stainless steel with special wax to clean and protect the finish.

COVERS

Winter covers should be safe, durable and sturdy. A good cover will last more than 10 years. A poly mesh stretch cover is the best. They connect to brass anchors mounted in the concrete. The stretch cover never needs cleaning and is very sturdy. The only draw back is small holes in the mesh will allow small dirt/debris particles to fall through into the pool. In the spring, you have to vacuum dirt/debris film on the bottom. Liner/marcite staining is commonly caused by this accumulation. To eliminate bottom dirt/debris film settling on the bottom, install an inexpensive cover under the poly mesh cover.

Vinyl covers are heavy-duty, durable and will last for 7 years. It must be cleaned every spring. Vinyl is the best insulating cover. It reduces chlorine dissipation. Using a vinyl cover is the best way to maintain crystal clear pool water through the winter months.

Regular solid covers work adequately. These covers are inexpensive, and could last for more than 8 yrs.. Solid covers must be supported with water tubes. Tubes must not be filled completely, or they could burst in the winter. Poly solid covers must be tied back to safely secure and maintain their original position. These covers can be somewhat troublesome: they can fall into the pool, rip and become undependable.

NOTES:

POOL EXCAVATING

Excavating must be well planned and executed. Using a larger machine will aid in accurately digging within the outside lines. Larger track machines can completely dig a pool in 3-6 hours. Smaller machines can dig a pool in 1-2 days. The amount of earth removed from a pool excavation is usually 80-160 cubic yards. Because there is so much dirt, it is best to haul away most of it and leave some for general purposes. For example, if your yard has low spots, if you want to elevate them or create berms, this earth can be utilized. Save most black dirt for landscaping uses later.

Of course, excavating is best accomplished when the ground is hard. Very soft ground can cause yard damage. Pool construction is very messy and a finished product requires patience and attention. Don't be upset if your backyard is slightly rough. Final grading and landscaping is essential to a well planned swimming pool area. It will restore your yard to a more beautiful area than it originally was.

To begin excavating, square and mark the outside pool configuration. Add 2 ft. to each side and end. Then stake, string, and paint. Use the design worksheets in this guide to plan your backyard. A finished pool will help you to decide on other landscaping options.

At the same time, excavate the concrete area; otherwise additional money will be spent later for extra concrete grading. Stake the concrete area and excavate as needed; then dig the swimming pool.

Squaring the pool may seem simplistic, and is mentioned throughout the text. It is, however, very important, and many mistakes are eliminated by proper squaring. If your swimming pool is not properly square (house-pool) the area can look somewhat different than intended. Planning, designing and improving the swimming pool area is best accomplished by establishing a workable site plan. The actual pool should again be checked for square to ensure a successful installation.

Excavating the concrete area first will provide a plan-link to other improvements. The deck size can be changed, if desired, and a curtain drain can be considered to re-route splash-water, rain, etc..

POOL EXCAVATING

Specification sheets are reviewed and transmitted to the swimming pool area. A good builder can excavate any soil conditions: soft black earth, hard clay, sand, gravel, etc.. Anticipate the possibility of underground water. Have some gravel (3/4 inch diameter) on site. When the deep end is completed, fill 6 inches with gravel, and insert a submersible pump with back flow valve. Be sure to over dig the deep end hopper (1-2) ft. to allow for gravel. Underground water isn't always a problem; usually in only 3 out of 10 jobs.

Soft sandy soil can undermine. Hand excavation is always required to shape the pool bottom. If you are in sand, hand excavating is a lot less work. Very hard clay can be handled with a pickax.

Most excavators know their job very well. Consult with them to understand their methods. Excavators usually have experience with new homes, trenches, sewer and water, and pools. Contact various excavators with experience in different areas.

You can use the excavator for digging, backfilling, gravel delivery,etc.. Be sure you understand his rates before he begins the work.

Backhoes are of several types; soft tire and track machines are the most common. The soft tire type is usually a smaller machine and will cost the most for work performed.

Track machines are very fast and best for pools. The track machine has roughly a 40 ft. reach and is very versatile. You can virtually position this machine outside the pool, and completely excavate the pool area. Before excavating, contact Diggers Hotline or underground utility companies to locate electric, phone, and gas. Within 48 hours they will mark all utilities with flags and paint. Locating utilities is part of planning your inground swimming pool. Your pool location should conform with local and state building codes. Check with your local building and zoning department.

Curtain drains can be installed to handle excessive rain and melting snow, otherwise water will saturate soil around the pool decking. A curtain drain will remove water from around the pool area, located beyond the concrete deck. Simply dig a trench around the deck, pitched to the lowest point of your yard. The water will collect and flow away from the pool area. Drains safeguard your concrete deck and pool. Melting snow in the spring can cause a lot of water damage and will flow back into the pool.

A curtain drain is merely a trench filled with gravel, and a black drainage tile installed. Inexpensive, and easy to install drains are a good way to protect your pool and landscaping. Locate a four inch gap between the decking and landscaping. Trench size can be 6, 8, or 12 inch. Backhoes or trenchers can be used. Always install after pouring the pool deck. I refer to the curtain drains as a maximum guard or MGP-system (maximum guard protection).

Pea-gravel is used for backfilling. Sand, river run, and crushed gravel can be installed as well. Sand should be spread even, and compacted every 16 inches of thickness. Sand is exceptional, providing a good base for the pool deck. Pea-stone is a clean, washed fill. It is a code-standard that doesn't settle or wash away. You must take care when backfilling not to damage the plumbing or pool. Sona-tubes can be installed at the pool perimeter to add an extra support for the pool decking.

The initial wall-grade level is excavated first; normally, 44.25 inches from a proposed top concrete grade. Simply use a transit to determine your concrete grade height, then add 44.25 to that measurement. The wall base should be level within 1 inch. Hand excavate to level within 1inch. Use the transit to attain the proper grade.

Next you must pin the exact pool inside the wall-area. Use a plumber's bob to square corners from the house and square to the shape.
To calculate squaring:
Example 16 X 32: 16 ft width x 32 ft length.
S=square measurement $=\sqrt{(W)^2 + (L)^2}$
S= $[(16)^2 + (32)^2]$ 1/2 $\triangleq$ 35.78 ft = 35'.9 1/3"
Simply a right triangle calculation:

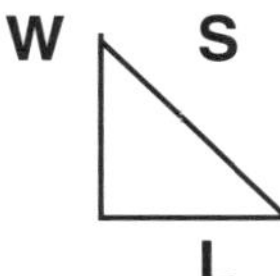

$S= \sqrt{W^2 = L^2}$

You can check the square lines extending from the sides of your home

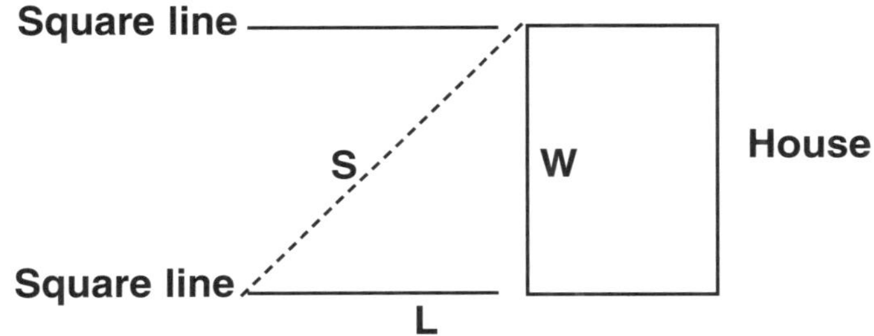

Square lines are used to exactly pinpoint a pool location. Simply position rebar in line with the side of your home. To check, use the right-triangle formula. The formula is derived from $a^2 + b^2 = c^2$. Width-a, length-b, c=square measurement.

Now you have pinned the exact pool location inside the hole. Stake and pin the deep end location. Your excavator can now dig that area. Once you have the deep end completed, you are ready to form footings or install wall panels.

You should use square lines before the pool area layout. You can position the line by eye and perfectly square the pool area by using the formula. Squaring is explained frequently throughout the text.

Reference pins should be positioned outside the pool area. Refer to page 105. Take extra care to retain their original position. Backhoe drivers should be instructed to avoid their locations. Also, instruct the driver to retain all outside pool lines. The major challenge to excavating is to prevent pool area layout position changes. The original position must always be maintained. The best way to be sure of original position is to hire a competent driver with a larger track machine. Once you have excavated the concrete area level, use the reference pins to locate the actual pool and work area. Then the work can be accurately performed and position retained.

Pre-planning the pool excavation will greatly aid in reducing digging time. Normally, machine operators charge by the hour. Improved planning and pinning will decrease the amount of expense and increase the pool position accuracy. An improved excavation will simplify panel/footing placement and installation. Use the pool specification sheets to transfer the pool to the proposed area.

(Liner/Concrete Pool) EXCAVATING

The excavator will first establish a initial grade for wall/footings placement. A flat area is excavated two ft. beyond the actual pool measurements. The grade level is usually 44 1/4 inches lower than the proposed concrete level. Simply add 44.25 inches to your transit stick measurement. Flat areas should be level to 1" after hand leveling.

Most excavators use a laser transit to level flat grade areas. The laser base unit is set and activated. The transit level mark is found and laser receiving unit attached to the grade stick. One man is required to hold the grade stick during excavations. You must be sure to grade the flat excavation area as accurately as possible.

Hand excavate the wall/footing area as needed to attain a constant grade to ± 1/2 inch. Use shovels, picks and a rake to accomplish a constant grade level.

Once you have reached a constant grade level the actual pool must be located inside the flat area. Use a tape measure and plumber's bob to locate the actual pool corners. A good way to locate pool corners is to position outside pins (reference points) outside the excavated area. Simply attach a string longer than the ends and sides and drive stakes to mark their locations:

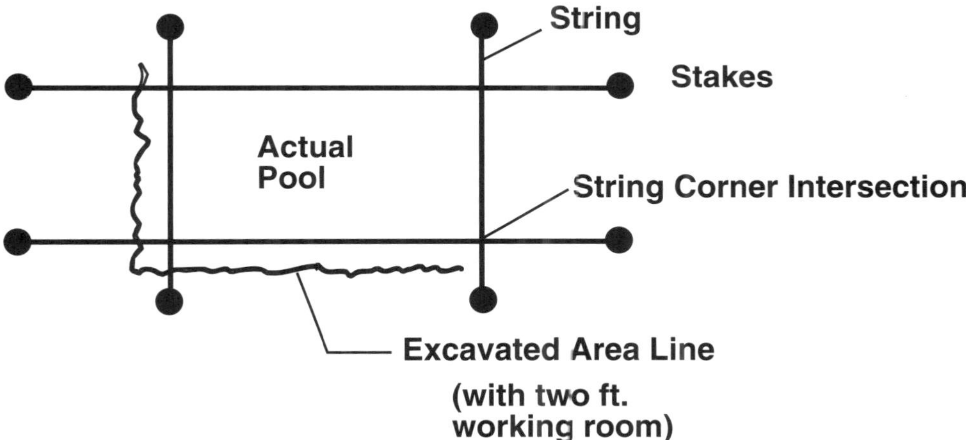

Utilizing this method, you can easily locate the actual pool corners. We call these stakes a point of reference. After the flat area is excavated, hold a plumber's bob at each string corner intersection.

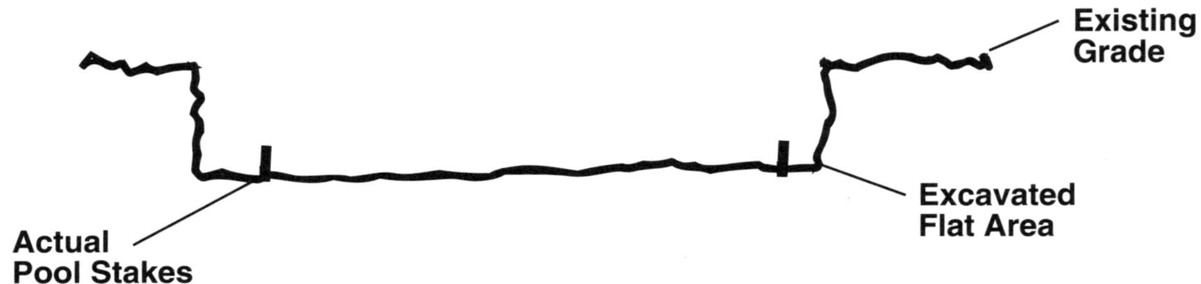

Now, attach strings to the actual pool stakes and paint pool lines. Next, measure the shallow end, incline and hopper from each end. Mark each location:

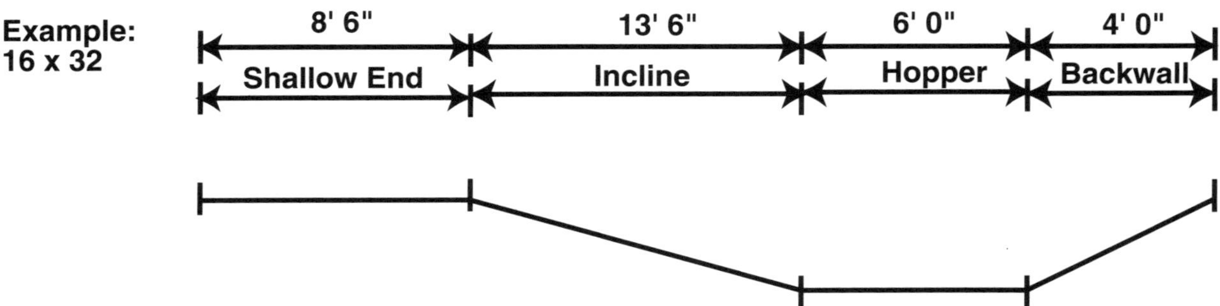

The excavator should be able to follow these stakes to properly dig the deep end. Hand digging is necessary to complete the deep area accurately. Use picks, shovels and a rake to hand excavate shallow end, incline, hopper and walls.

Hand dig the shallow end flat. Remove any extra earth from the wall/footing area. The shallow area is very easy to excavate and should be finished quickly. The 4 hopper pins should be located at the deepest area. Position a stake at the shallow end/incline corner. Attach a string from this stake to a hopper pin:

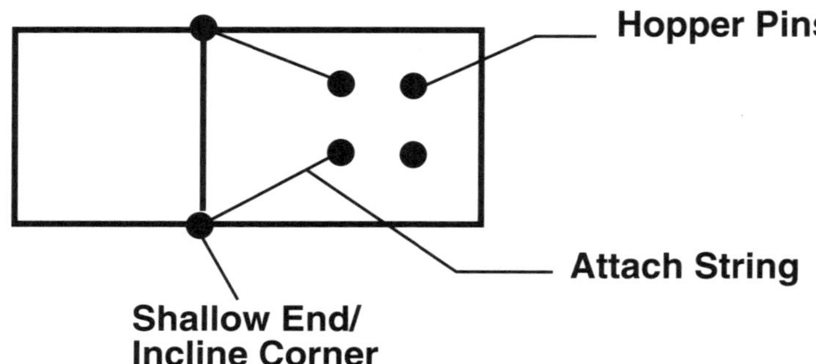

These areas should be hand picked and shoveled until the string is stretched tight and level. Dig 2 inches below the string level to install form boards for pool base.(liner pool)

The hopper should be prepared depending on the pool installed. This area must be over dug 1-2 feet lower to contain gravel and control potential water problems. A main drain and french drain will be installed. You must prepare the deep area for these pool components. Simply dig a trench 1 X 1 X 1 ft. into the side wall.

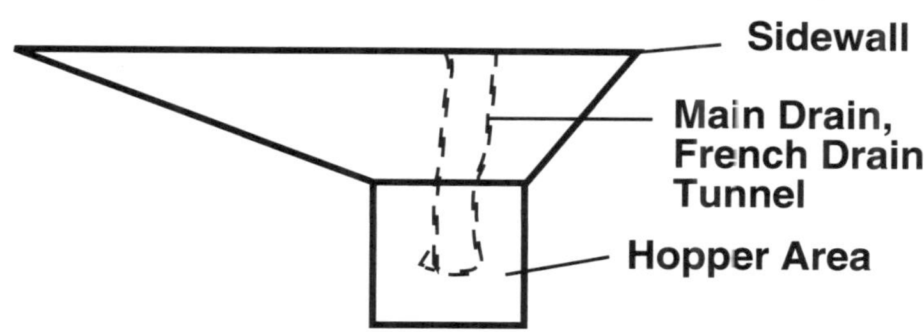

In this trench, install two plastic poly pipes (100 psi) for the main drain and french drain. Remove all extra earth taken from the pool bottom. A good way to remove excess dirt is to use buckets attached to a large diameter rope. When the pool bottom is completely hand excavated, install the wall panels. The panels are placed in the 2 ft. work area and installed according to pool specification sheets.

After hand excavating, a small amount of gravel should be installed at the shallow and incline areas. This will keep the pool bottom work area clean and dry.

Rain and adverse weather conditions can cause mud and soil erosion. A sloppy pool area can cause a builder frustration and expense. Always use gravel to improve the pool area workability. Rain delays are common and should be taken into consideration. Dry weather is preferred for excavating and installing footing/panels. Large tarps can be used as covering for the pool area to improve work after a heavy rain. Purchase inexpensive rain covering at a local building store. If you fail to use a tarp, the pool construction must be delayed until the area dries.

POOL EXCAVATING (Concrete)

When excavating a concrete pool, the initial pool bottom must be excavated 9 inches below the finished concrete grade to allow for four inches of gravel and five inches of concrete. Also the footing area must be excavated, and forms set as explained in the concrete pool construction section. A perfectly excavated inground pool will decrease the amount of work and increase pool life.

If water is found while excavating, continue to dig the deep area. Overdig the hopper area 2 feet. Install .75 inch gravel and insert a submersible pump with back flow valve to remove water as needed. A french drain will be installed later to remove water and keep the construction area dry. A french drain is a foot valve installed into the 2 ft. of gravel. By attaching a poly pipe from a pump to the valve, a water suction is created, removing excess water from the hopper work area. The pump, of course, must be turned on and off. The french drain can be routed to the actual pool pump, removing ground water, and filling your pool acting as a shallow well. Once your pool is filled with water, the french drain is no longer needed because of the hydrostatic water pressure on the pool bottom. If the pool is concrete, a hydrostatic valve may be installed in the main drain to release underground water into the pool's water supply.

French drains are installed just in front of the main drain. Both pool components use the same trench, as explained previously. Installing the main drain is delicate, and proper procedure must be used. Simply, attach the main drain unit to a poly pipe (100 psi. 1.5 inch diameter.) Heat,glue, and double clamp the male poly fitting inserted in the main drain. There is a main drain diagram in the function section.

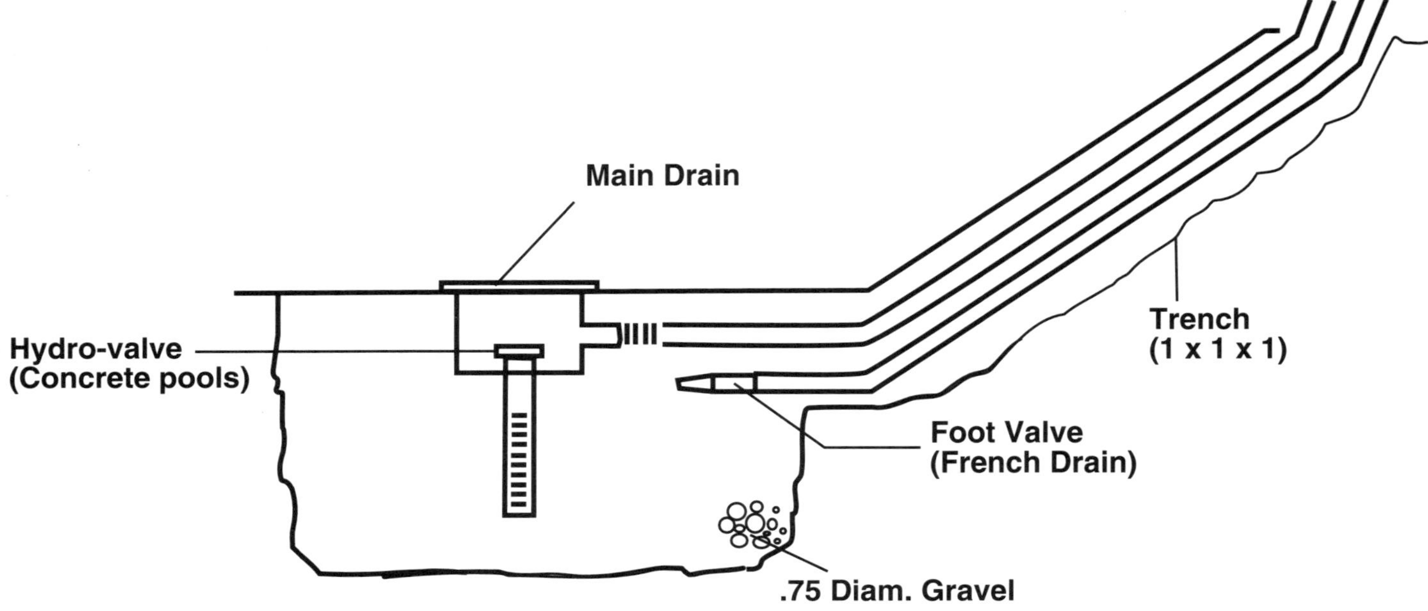

Underground plumbing is an important part of every inground swimming pool. Different materials are installed; Poly pipe 80-200 psi, Spa hose, and PVC pipe. Mostly poly pipe is used because of the material strength and durability. This pipe is somewhat flexible and very strong. Thickness is roughly 1/8 inch at 100 psi. Poly pipe is economical and easily purchased. This pipe will last for years because of the added expansion/contraction feature. Most poly pipe doesn't fracture when exposed to extreme temperature differences. Most fractures occur at the plastic fittings. Residential pools have mostly poly pipe plumbing.

PVC pipe is used for commercial pools (state code). Most of these pools are located indoors. PVC pipe will fracture very easily when exposed to very cold temperatures. (Not recommended for residential pools)
Spa hose is very flexible and durable but the cost is prohibitive.

Poly pipe is available in 100 ft rolls. It is a large roll with a five foot diameter. To install, simply unroll the pipe in the trench. Poly pipe is heated, glued, and double clamped. Care must be taken to install the connections properly. Male fittings are installed at the inlets and many types of connectors are available; nineties, tees, females, and reducers are a few. Connectors must be high pressure and high quality. The pipe is easily cut with a hack saw. The best way to protect the underground plumbing is to install antifreeze for winterizing. To calculate the amount of RV, figure the area of pipe to be filled; $\pi/4\ d^2 l$: where d=diameter, l=length. Example: 100 ft of pipe, diameter= 1.5 inches. $\pi/4\ (.125)^2\ (100) \hat{=}\ 1.23\ ft^3$; and 7.4 gallons of antifreeze fills the volume of 1.0 ft^3. So roughly 9.1 gallons are needed. Antifreeze will protect the poly piping to –50 degrees Fahrenheit. RV is added as a sure method for 100% protection. Be sure all plumbing lines are completely full.

PVC pipe is installed above the ground at the control slab. The slab contains the pump, filter and heater. High pressure fittings are used (schedule 40), to avoid leaks. Brass gate valves are installed to control skimmers, inlets and main drain. Be sure to label these valves with a marker.

You can easily install an automatic chlorinator when pvc pipe is used above ground. Simply drill holes after the pump and heater. This installation procedure is for an off-line chlorinator. In-line chlorinators are plumbed directly after the heater water flow. Chlorinators direct the chlorine water flow back into the pool.

Before underground plumbing 12 inches of backfill material is poured to protect the pipe from the rough concrete footing.

ELECTRIC WORK

An important part of all pool building is the electric work. (Most electric work should be performed by a licensed electrician). We will explain the various work that should be included. Pool pumps are factory wired 115 and 220 volts. The lower voltage is chosen to extend the motor life.

Installation/material costs are less when using the 115 volts. Pool bonding (grounding) is necessary to protect the pool and homeowner. Bonding is relatively simple. A ground wire is connected to any metal in or near the swimming pool. When constructing concrete/gunite; rebar, mesh, ladders, handrails and lights are bonded to a ground rod. Liner pool steel walls are bonded, along with handrails, ladders, etc.. Usually the sockets have wire connectors. The real important trick is to never use a copper–steel contact surface. This will cause oxidation, and the connection will not last. Connectors should be aluminum and installed permanently.

Bonding is required on all swimming pools and should be inspected by local building and zoning. Most electric lines require a GFI (Ground fault Interrupter). One to two lines are required and the electric code is strictly enforced. Pool lights should be 115 volts, and a 12 volt transformer installed. Pool niches and assemblies are explained in previous sections. Niches are aluminum and lights are approved. Most work must be inspected and proper procedure is required.

Convenience outlets and pool lights (12 volt systems) are installed near the pool area. Different color lights are attractive and functional. At any rate, the use of 24 hour timers is popular and frequently implemented. Timers allow you to automatically run the pump, filter, auto-cleaners, etc.. Seven day timers are also available.

Electrical work must be perfect and in accordance to local, state and national codes. Codes may vary from state to state. Be sure to hire a competent licensed electrician to complete the work needed.

Concrete Work

The following are details to help you understand concrete inground pool construction. Concrete is used for structures, driveways and finished walkways. Structural concrete is used for all buildings applications.

Inground pools utilize concrete walls, footings and walkways. Concrete work becomes very important when constructing inground pools. Gunite pools are a special grade of concrete which is applied with air pressure. Shot-crete pools are a lot like gunite.

Concrete completely cures after 14 days. The weight of concrete can actually fracture the material. Roads fracture one day after they are poured. Expansion joints are saw cut and the concrete fractures at the joints. This only applies to concrete thickness 8-12 inches. Most concrete reaches a strength of 5,000 psi, which is extremely strong.

Concrete work cures very evenly at room temperature (68°). At warmer temperatures concrete cures at an accelerated rate, and at lower temperatures concrete cures at a decelerated rate. Concrete should cure evenly at the optimum temperature. Additives, accelerators and hot water are added to the concrete mix when outside temperatures are lower. Chloride is a common accelerator.

When Chloride is added, line traces are visible on the finished concrete surface. The best conditions can be simulated with heat instead of using additives or accelerators.

Underground footings usually are 5 bag cement mix. Larger stones (3/4" diameter) are used. Patio mix concrete is 6 Bag cement mix with smaller stones.

Pouring a patio must be carefully planned to maximize the best job possible. Ideally, the temperature should be 60-80°F, and you should use a reputable concrete supply company. When pouring concrete, use ready mix companies. Never attempt to mix your own; you will not save any money, in fact you will cause yourself a lot of unnecessary work and trouble.

Concrete footings for pools should be a constant thickness. Ground excavation should be uniform and gravel thickness constant. Forms can be used and should be installed whenever possible. Footings should be rough finished with a trowel or flat shovel. They are used for concrete walls, brick retaining walls and securing pool walls. Level, square and according to manufacturer's specs, pour a 6-10 inch thick footing around the walls to properly lock in the panels. Rebar should be used to secure walls to ground locations. If the walls are not properly secured before pouring footings, they may move because of the concrete pressure.

Steel/foam wall footings can be installed and will lock in walls permanently. Footings can be poured or troweled and can be used for many applications. Finished footings should be inspected by the Building/Zoning departments for proper approval.

Flat work is more delicate and requires an experienced finisher. Concrete finishers usually are very good with 10 years of experience. Never attempt to do your own flatwork. You can very easily ruin what should be a very nice job. However, you can form and prepare flat work for a finisher.

When forming flat work, pitch the concrete 1/4 inch per linear foot. If your pool deck is 4 ft wide a 1 inch pitch is necessary. Set 1 x 4's or 2 x 4's level and square, at the desired width.

Install four inches of pea-gravel before pouring any flat work. The additional gravel will aid in eliminating concrete fractures. The gravel provides a direction for water to flow, preventing the water from contacting the concrete. Water-concrete contact may cause fractures and deterioration. The gravel also provides a very suitable curing environment. Most zoning departments require 4 inches of gravel. Concrete work may stand up better to ground shifting and movement as well with a base of gravel.

Before pouring a patio, pool deck, or sidewalk; install wire mesh and rebar to strengthen the concrete slab. Rebar and wire mesh must be bonded (connected to a ground rod). Usually #8 bare copper wire is installed, and ground rod connectors used.

When pouring any flat work, proper preparations are mandatory. Be sure you are completely ready to pour. Cover any pool parts with duct tape: ladders, handrails, skimmers, concrete finish edges, etc.. Then level the concrete as you pour by skreeting. A straight 2 x 4 works well. You must rough trowel as you pour. **IMPORTANT**: your finished concrete work will remain the same shape as you have leveled and rough troweled.

Rough troweling is the most important step to a properly finished deck. Edges are troweled in and expansion joints can be installed with a trowel as well. The best concrete contractors use a counter-joint trowel attached to aluminum poles.

Finish troweling is accomplished by using a flat metal trowel. Water must not be sprayed on the concrete surface because it will reduce the strength on the finished surface. Chipping and cracking may occur if water is sprayed on while finishing.

A smooth concrete surface can easily be attained. The best way to guarantee a perfect job is to hire a couple of experienced finishers for the actual concrete pour.

Expansion joints should be located and marked with a black marker. Use strings to insure perfectly straight joints. If pre-marked, the finishers can simply snap a line and install the joint. Joints actually section off the concrete work and provide a better concrete finish.

Concrete is both functional and visual. Finished concrete enhances and complements a swimming pool layout. Other types of concrete can be used: Kool Deck, Exposed Aggregate, etc..

Exposed Aggregate is nice looking and will provide a long lasting deck material. There are several types of exposed aggregate. You can visit your local concrete company for different samples.

FALL/WINTER CONSTRUCTION

Pools can be constructed in the fall and winter months. Special care must be exercised to install the inground pool properly. Your attitude will be more relaxed because the work does not have to be completed at a certain deadline or rushed for swimming weather.

Fall is the best time to save money on the pool and all the components. Workers in the construction trades are usually slow and could use the extra work. You can save a lot of money on materials, labor and machine operations.

There are many advantages to fall construction. The ground is usually hard due to the long, dry summer. Trucks and machines will not damage the yard as much. The ground water table is lower, so construction is easier.

The swimming pool is the biggest part of the project. The best thing to do is construct the swimming pool in the fall and complete the concrete work in the spring. Concrete work and landscaping can easily be completed and doesn't require as much time.

Your pool will be completed and in place for years to come. Don't rush the project. If you hire a competent builder he still may have problems with adverse weather conditions. Be understanding and kind to pool builders. Don't pressure him for completion. Instead, aim for a proper installation.

MISC. CONSTRUCTION TIPS

Constructing an inground pool is a time-consuming project. It demands expertise, flexibility, and attention to detail. Never try to rush the project. Allow enough time for each phase to be completed properly and safely. Prepare your timetable with all these considerations in mind.

Fall construction is both fun and rewarding. Temperatures are usually moderate, and workers comfortable. The atmosphere is relaxed and conditions are favorable.

Winter pool construction is possible. Many builders work until Christmas. Heaters and tarps are used. Make sure clean burning heat is used for safer construction. Kerosene torpedo heaters are dangerous and should not be used. Natural gas heaters can be used if available.

The cost of winter construction is sometimes higher and many builders don't work. However, I have constructed inground pools during winter, and enjoy the conditions.

The cost of an inground pool should be amortized over the duration of time you live at a residence. The pool is enjoyed and maintained for years, and adds value to your property. Financing is available.

Completing an inground pool prior to spring is smart and will prepare you for concrete work and landscaping. The pool area can be heated so that work can be completed comfortably. Many builders work in the off-season and costs can be lower.

NEW CONSTRUCTION

POOL

Pool Size: ______________________________

Pool Style: ______________________________

Pool Bottom: ______________________________

Wall: ______________________________

Deck Support System: ______________________________

Finish edge at concrete: ______________________________

FILTRATION SYSTEM: ______________________________

Pump: ______________________________

Pool Type: ______________________________

Maintenance Kit: ______________________________

Timer: ______________________________

Auto Chlorinator: ______________________________

Ladders: ______________________________

Handrails: ______________________________

Automatic cleaner: ______________________________

Heater: ______________________________

Diving Board: ______________________________

Stairs: ______________________________

Light: ______________________________

Transformer: ______________________________

Slide: ______________________________

Solar Cover: ______________________________

Chemicals: ______________________________

Cover: ______________________________

Other: ______________________________

Other: ______________________________

New pool construction must be carefully planned and carefully done. There are many topics to consider. So far we have mentioned utilities, positions, grade elevation, retaining walls, design/planning, control centers and berms. We will thoroughly discuss these and a few others.

Position is determined by land layout, pool size, shape and available swimming pool area. As previously mentioned, avoid utilities, septic systems and wells to eliminate the expense of moving them. The electric/phone lines can be relocated by the power company or a licensed electrician. Cost is usually from $300 to $1200. If a proposed pool area conflicts with power lines, relocating is necessary. Above ground lines can be moved free of charge. Underground lines must also be routed away from the pool area at the owner's expense. It is common to move existing utility lines.

Locate all septic fields. Two to three lines can be sealed and new lines rerouted at a cost of $500 to $1500, but because relocation of septic lines is expensive, you can save money by avoiding this. Septic tanks and wells should never be moved because of the prohibitive expense, unless the old systems need replacing.

Pool position is commonly parallel or perpendicular to the house. A good practice is to use the house as a reference point to square the pool to the house because the house is usually very square. Utilizing the house end as a pool concrete edge helps to organize the pool construction area. Many use the house end for the start of a fence. However, offsetting the fence is preferred.

Choose a pool shape you really like. Most shapes are available in many sizes. As mentioned, the 16 x 32 ft. pool is the industry standard size, and accessories, components, repairs, and operating costs are fairly low. Larger pools are more expensive to open, winterize, install, repair and operate. There are certain economical alternatives to larger pools. One is the 20 x 32 Grecian, featuring a reduced pool area with increased width. It is an attractive pool.

Sun position is relatively important. Consider locating the pool away from large trees to prevent sunlight block. Avoiding large trees will also decrease pool maintenance by eliminating leaves, seeds and debris from entering the pool water.

It is sometimes necessary to remove trees from the pool area. Smaller trees, bushes and other foliage can be replanted elsewhere in the yard. Improved sunlight access will help to heat the pool. However, more sunlight will dissipate pool chemicals rapidly. Consider some shade to reduce the effect of summer warmth. Most experienced pool owners rarely heat the pool. In fact, they allow the summer weather to provide plenty of warm pool temperatures. Solar covers can greatly aid in heating the pool and preventing heat loss. Pool covers are inexpensive and also improve pool conditions.

Many pool builders consider prevailing wind direction when positioning pools. Although it is an accepted rule to locate skimmers toward the most common wind direction, we prefer to locate skimmers at the house side for added convenience.

Operating the filter system is recommended from 12:00 midnight to 5:00 am., when wind direction is rarely a factor. Early morning operation will prepare the pool for each new day and decrease electric bills.

The best way to position a pool is to consider the house, existing patios, landscaping, etc.. Draw a site plan with focus on improved appearance.

Consider a shaded area addition from the house for non-swimming pool loungers...a social area for cooking out, parties, etc.. An inground pool is a home extension and complements the area. Most homeowners position the pool for an improved view from the home.

Wooden decks beyond the pool area are frequently installed. Usually the house floor is elevated and many homes already have an existing wooden deck on the same level. The best way to mesh an existing deck with a new deck on the level of the pool area is to simply insert stairs leading to the pool deck. This patio area can be utilized in conjunction with the pool deck. A concrete sidewalk can be installed to mesh existing decks and pool walkways.

A lounge area can be installed near the pool. Extend the pool deck 8-12 ft. on one side and one end. The other side and end can be 4-6 ft..

Plan fencing with a design to suit the pool area. An existing fence may be incorporated into this design. For added safety, many homeowners include a fence around the pool area. However, this is not mandatory. There are many fence styles to choose from. The basic fence materials are:

1. Wood **3. Aluminum**
2. PVC **4. Steel**

Wood fences are durable, sturdy and economical. Sanding, staining and painting are required. Consider treated wood in 1/2 to 3/4 inch thickness. The most popular style is called dog-ear. Available in many types of wood, these are privacy fences, ranging from 4-6 ft. in height. They are functional as well, blocking unwanted winds. Visit a lumber yard or look at existing fences to make the selection best suited to your needs. I have designed the following inexpensive treated fence. (material cost: $300.00)

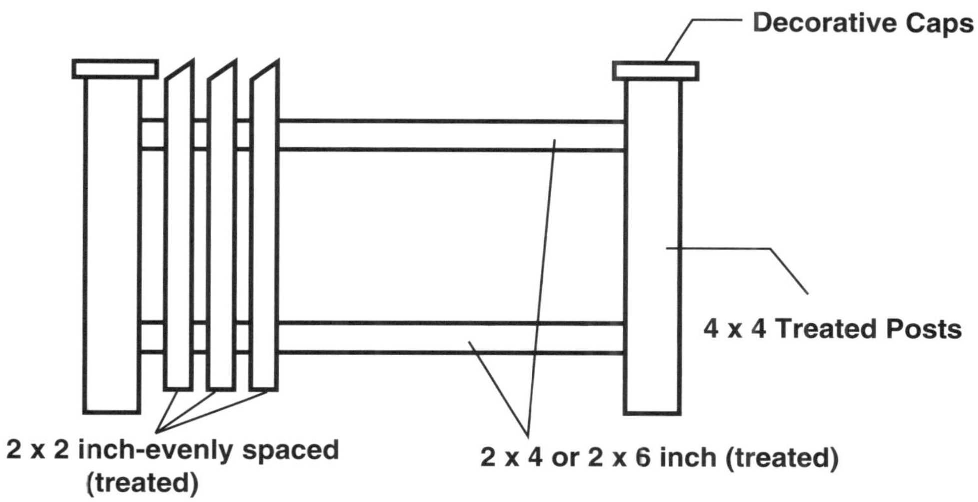

This fence is practical and functional. It is positioned at the pool deck edge, complete with two 4 ft. gates. First, set 4 x 4 posts in concrete on 6 ft. centers, then attach a horizontal double row of rails (either 2 x 4's or 2 x 6's). Next attach vertical 2 x 2 slats, spacing them according to local zoning requirements. The finished pool fence is attractive, yet relatively inexpensive.

PVC fences are fairly new and somewhat expensive. The popular stable fence is installed everywhere. PVC plastic may weather, so it is not always recommended.

The best and most popular fence is the non-maintenance aluminum rod-iron style. It never needs painting or replacing. Durable extruded aluminum, shown on the cover, lasts for years without repair. Available in brown, black or white, this great looking fence features an extended 30 yr. or lifetime warranty. There are many styles to choose from. Installation cost is usually low, but material costs are relatively expensive.

Cyclone fences, presently coated with brown or black plastic, are decorative and functional. They are attractive and will complement any pool area. Moderately priced, they blend well with bushes and landscaping.

Machine access is important when constructing an inground pool. Try to avoid entrance from the driveway. Large excavating machines, dump trucks and concrete trucks should enter from a house side. Yard damage is to be expected and will be repaired upon completion of the project. Never drive concrete trucks on thin asphalt driveways. The asphalt should be at least three inches thick. Back the truck slowly and observe the drive. Concrete can be pumped or wheeled to the rear yard from the street. When ordering concrete, instruct the ready mix plant to send a smaller truck. This will improve access.

If a field or vacant lot is near, contact the owner and ask permission to use it to access your site. Field access is common and most owners will allow you to drive on their land.

Temporary fences are sometimes required during pool construction. They are inexpensive and readily available at most building stores. Usually orange or red, they are a safety protection for homeowners. Check with the local building and zoning departments for requirements.

New inground pool construction inspections are mandatory. Contact the local inspector for inspection at each phase of construction. Depending on where you live, inspections are made before the concrete footing, backfilling, concrete work and a final inspection after completion. Electrical work is separate and must also be inspected. A 24-48 hr... notice is required, so arrange your timetable to schedule these inspections.

Sump pump lines should be extended and rerouted. Connect a 90° PVC fitting elbow and install poly pipe underground, away from the pool area. Existing drain tiles can be eliminated and new pipe installed. Sump pump lines may cause soil erosion and saturation near the pool deck and area, causing problems later.

LAKESIDE POOLS

Inground pools are frequently situated near lakes, ponds, streams, etc., providing a unique setting. The pool area is normally built into a hill or a slight downward slope. Special care and procedure are necessary. When excavating, ground water will be encountered at a very shallow depth, sometimes 3-5 ft.. The best way to control ground water is to install a drainage system trench around the pool area. Simply dig a 2 ft. wide trench pitched at .50 inch per ft., install .75 diam... washstone and place drainage tile in trench. Backfill with gravel. You may excavate the pool area first. For example, lay out the pool size, concrete and landscape area, then grade the area flat. Then install the drainage system trench, (DST), and proceed with the pool. Be sure the DST is excavated to extend well below the final deep end grade.

DST SYSTEM

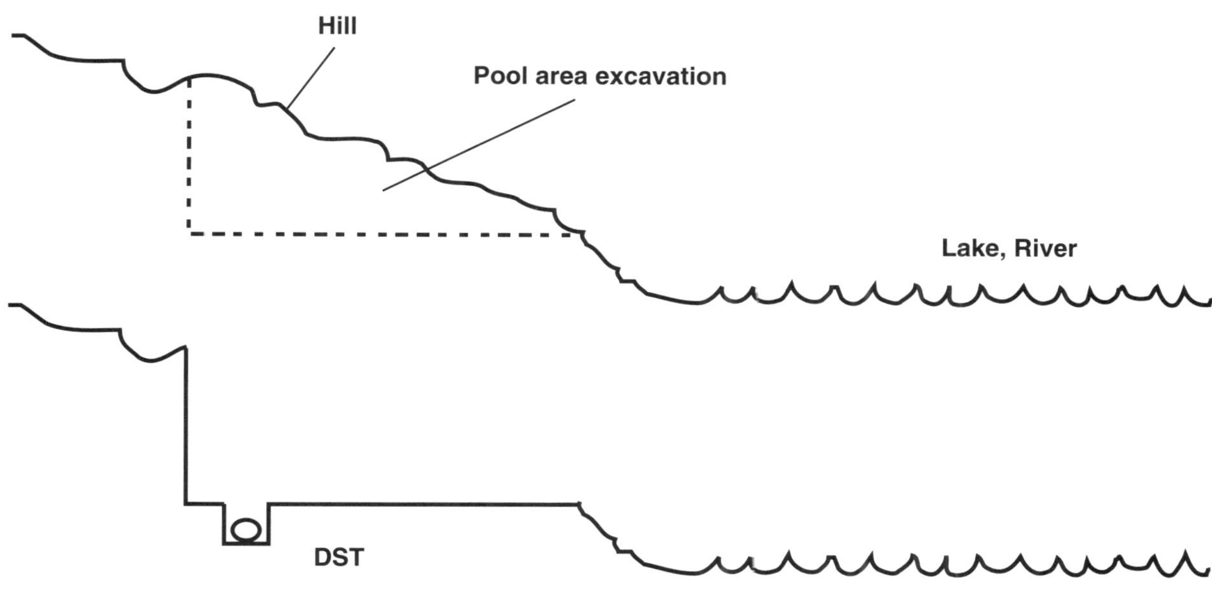

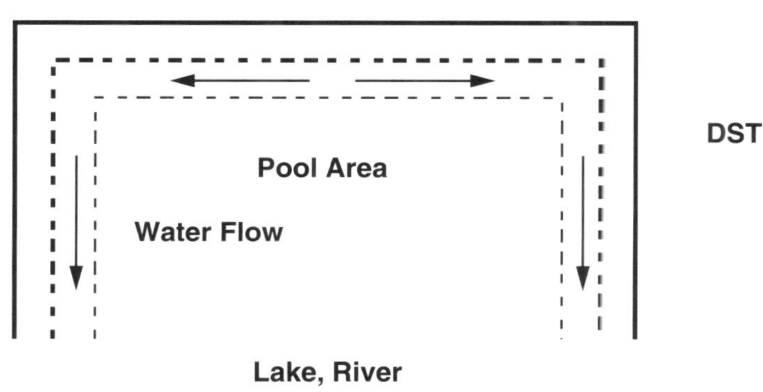

The DST will reroute ground water into the lake or river, providing a dryer pool excavation. A DST will operate for years because most ground water flows to underground creeks and other waterways. A 2 ft. trench will adequately reroute most water. A french drain is then installed, as explained in previous sections.

The remaining challenge is to prevent ground undermining. Undermining is common because of very soft soil conditions. Sand is usually present at the 3-6 ft. level. To prevent undermining, under-dig the pool deep end sides, and back wall. Overdig the hopper 2 ft. and install gravel and a submersible pump. Then, install a french drain to handle water easily. Upon pool completion, connect the french drain to the filter system and use the ground water to fill the pool. Complete the pool installation and landscaping.

When little or no slope exists, the pool must be elevated. Most earth excavated will be used for backfilling and sona-tubes should be installed along with gravel every 4-6 ft. as previously explained in the pool excavation section. A DST should be considered for this situation as well.

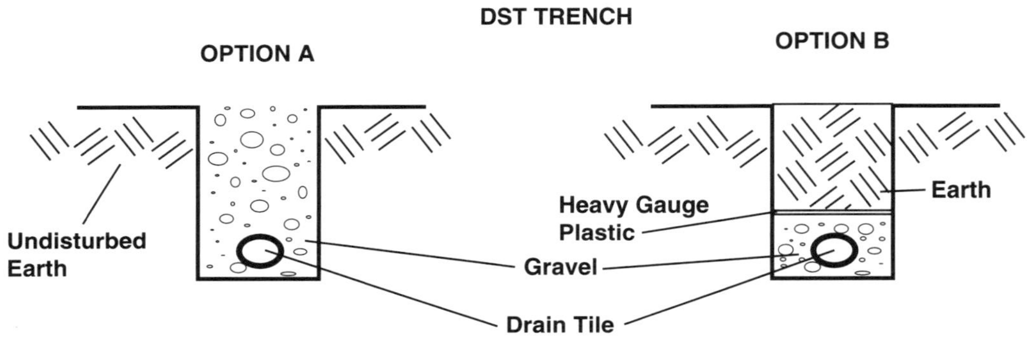

Option A will reroute melting snow and rain as well. Option B will only reroute ground water.

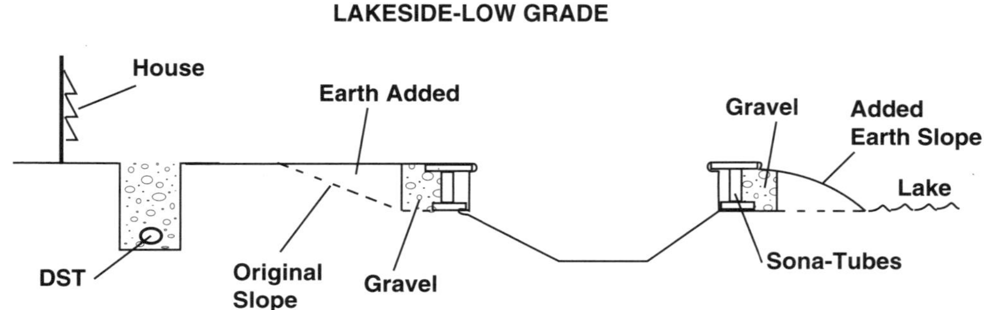

Pools that are properly installed require little or no repair within the first 10 years; however if there is a problem, solutions can be easily implemented. Leaks rarely occur and can be easily fixed. The following are different leaks and solutions:

MOST COMMON:

1. **Filter/pump**
2. **Above ground plumbing**
3. **Heater**

LEAST COMMON:

1. **Light**
2. **Underground Plumbing**
3. **Pool Leaks**

Usually leaks occur at the pump/filter. Visually inspect the pump and filter. Replace O-rings, seals, etc. to fix leaks. Check the water connections and the plumbing near the pump. The pump is the functional force which will cause leaks because it generates high pressure. Most high pressure occurs after the pump. Therefore most leaks can be located in that region. Seals, plastic, and filter/heater components can be damaged by the combination of high pressure and aging parts. Refer to the winterizing section for proper maintenance to extend the life of the pump/filter and heater.

When plumbing leaks occur, check all water connections. When replacing pvc pipe, install high pressure fittings, silicone and teflon tape. It is easy to fix and replace above ground plumbing. Check valves for leaks; the best valves are brass ball or regular brass. Plastic valves will weather and not last very long.

Heater leaks can be easily fixed. Check the water connections and plumbing. Most leaks occur at the water headers. (Refer to the section on heaters) Remove water headers, and replace as needed. Usually, water headers have a large rubber gasket and 6-8 bolts.

Simply remove the exterior heater panels and unbolt the water headers. Replace the header and gaskets as needed. Locate wires and draw a diagram to aid you in reassembly. The water connections are located on the right side header. Check the large rubber seals and replace as needed. Left side headers are closed with only a single petcock to remove air/water from the heater. Petcocks can easily be removed/installed. Petcocks turn opposite normal threads and are easily replaced.

Pool light niche assemblies rarely leak. There is a possibility that the light conduit is fractured. You can easily seal the pipe from inside the pool. Simply lower the water level well below the light assembly, and seal the light cord/conduit with silicone. Windshield seal can be installed first to provide a primary seal, then apply silicone to ensure a secondary bond. Complete the repair and allow the silicone to cure. If the niche assembly leaks, a new niche may be installed. To install a new niche assembly; lower the water level below the niche and saw cut a two foot strip in the pool deck. Then hand excavate the backfill material below the niche assembly. Remove the old niche and install a new one. Be sure to install a heavy wall plastic conduit. Reposition the old faceplate and seal with silicone. Reinsert the light and connect the wires in the junction box. Backfill the repair area and install new concrete .(Important: a licensed electrician may be required to reconnect the junction box wiring)

Underground plumbing rarely fractures if properly installed and winterized. (Refer to the winterizing section) To determine a leak/fracture in the underground plumbing, install plugs in the inlet fittings and skimmers. Be sure to lower the pool water level below the inlets and skimmers. Apply teflon tape and silicone to threaded plugs and install them in the inlets and skimmers. Fill the pool to normal operating level and wait to determine if the pool is leaking. If the pool isn't leaking, then your problem is in the underground plumbing. To determine which line is leaking, remove skimmer plugs first, then inlet plugs. Another way to determine underground plumbing fractures is to pressure test each line. Install plugs at each line and apply compressed air. Use a pressure gauge to determine a loss of pressure over a period of time.

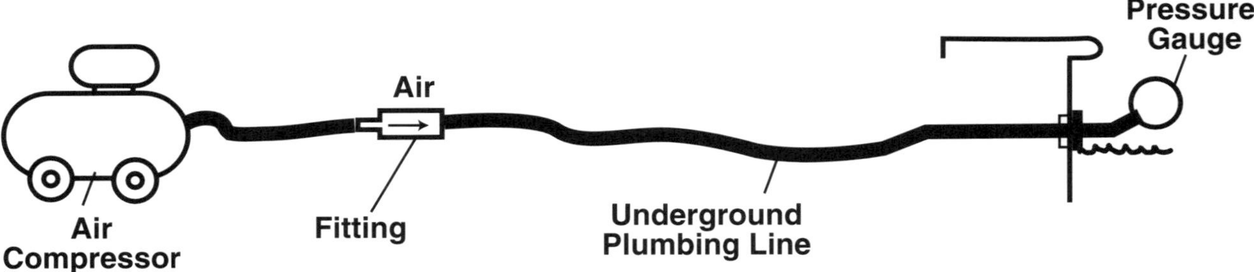

Pool leaks located at the bottom and sides are rare. The best way to find a structural leak is visually. Have a scuba diver check the pool interior. Leaks are easily spotted and repaired. Liner pools can be patched underwater. When patching a liner pool underwater, clean the surface and apply a patch with underwater glue. Apply pressure with a weight, and leave it until the glue drys. The best patch is made with an exact matching liner pattern sample. Cut the patch one inch larger in diameter than the tear. Apply enough glue neatly, and use enough weight to hold the patch firmly. Underwater repairs should be checked once a year to be sure they remain sealed. A good way to be sure is to reseal the patch once a year. Above water repairs are easy and do not have to be checked later.
Gunite/Concrete pools can be patched and resurfaced. You must remove all water from the pool and repair as needed. Marcite/pool paint is removed by sandblasting, and the interior sealed. A new coat of Marcite/pool paint is applied and pool refilled. Most pools do not require repair within the first 10 years if properly installed. You can repair and resurface the pool after 8 years to prevent future problems. Pool leaks require water pressure to leak. Without pressure, leaks do not occur. Upon removing water the pressure at your leak will decrease; thus, most leaks are at or near the pool water level. You can let the pool lose water until the leaking stops. The decrease in water loss may direct you to the exact leak location.
Liner pools rarely leak if properly installed. Sidewall patching is common and easily repaired. Lower the water level three inches below the leak, apply a matching patch and position a second patch behind the front patch. Duct tape the rear patch, and the repair is complete.This is called a lifetime patch and may outlast the original liner.

At any rate, a liner at least 10 years old should be replaced. If you do not replace it, leaks may occur and repair costs will be more than the cost of a new liner. New liners are inexpensive and can be easily made to fit your pool perfectly. If you are considering a new liner then you should replace key pool components like skimmers, maindrains, inlets, plumbing lines,etc.. This is called inground swimming pool rebuilding. Refer to the pool bottom section to identify key pool measurements needed to ensure a perfect liner fit. I have supplied a pool rebuilding section to help you ensure a well-fitting liner, 100 percent wrinkle-free.

If you have a new liner installed, please insist on a written guarantee of satisfaction that it will fit properly and be 100 percent wrinkle-free. A liner which is too small or ill-fitting will cause major problems, detaching itself and becoming an eyesore.

Pool liners should be a minimum of 20 mils thickness and manufactured by a reputable company. Seams must be electronically sealed and an anti-bacterial film applied. Inground liners are high quality, and will last for years with proper maintenance. Refer to the chemical and maintenance section for extended liner life.

Pool liners are available in white/blue base colors. White is usually the best color, because oxidation from pool chemicals will not show fading and discoloration.

There are certain pool chemicals which claim they do not fade or deteriorate pool liners. Such claims are not always true because of the high intensity of sunlight and liner material specifications.

The best way to ensure your liner will last for years is to use a white base liner with a selected print and maintain the pool properly. Your pool should always be clean and have a proper chemical concentration.

Concrete/gunite pools with a white marcite bottom show little or no fading. The only problem that may occur is staining.

Stains can be removed after your pool is properly shocked. Usually 7-14 days is required for the stain to disappear. Stains are common after winter. Upon opening your swimming pool, you may find a few stains. Don't vigorously brush the pool bottom to remove stains. You must oxidize the pool water and bottom with shock.

A common problem with marcite is a brown discoloration. Again shock the pool and the discoloration should be removed. If not, the the marcite may have to be replaced. Usually marcite 9 years old or older shows some discoloration.

Concrete pools with a painted bottom require an acid bath every one to two years. Muriatic acid is used. Extreme caution should be taken because of the harmful fumes. Important: Do not attempt this yourself. Hire a pool builder to apply acid baths.

You should have acid baths completed by a competent pool builder. Acid baths are inexpensive and remove most staining. Painted pool stains are not easily removed. An acid bath will usually remove them.

Liner pool stains are usually removed easily. Stains are common after winter, and again, shocking the pool should remove all stains. A liner pool has a thin anti-bacterial film applied at the factory and most dirt, algae, and debris slide right off the vinyl. Liner pools require the least maintenance and are preferred because of a lower building cost. Many people who have owned concrete pools will advise you to buy a liner because of lower cleaning and repair costs. The worst repair that can occur is replacing the pool liner and replacement costs are low. Liner pools should be rebuilt and repairs planned carefully before a liner is replaced.

Liner Pool Rebuilding

There are 10 things to consider when rebuilding or replacing the pool liner.

Condition of:
1. **Pool walls**
2. **Liner**
3. **Concrete finish edge**
4. **Pool bottom**
5. **Skimmers**
6. **Inlets**
7. **Main Drain**
8. **Underground Plumbing**
9. **Pool Deck**

Rebuilding the liner pool is both fun and rewarding. You can hire a pool builder to execute the repairs or you can do the work yourself. The following are details of complete liner pool rebuilding.

Rebuilding starts with a very thorough visual inspection. If your pool is at least 10 years old, replacing vital components will be necessary.

First, check the concrete edge, (liner bead receiver). Its finish edge should be aluminum. If the bead receiver is plastic you may want to install a new white aluminum extruded assembly. Many people use a plastic strip mounted just below the existing concrete receiver. This is inexpensive, and does not require any pool deck cutting or replacing.

Plastic bead receivers usually weather and crack after 10 years. A new aluminum receiver will add to pool life. To install a new receiver, cut your pool deck 6-10 inches from the inside of the pool wall. Remove the concrete and detach the old plastic bead receiver. Install the new aluminum finish edge and drill into walls with self-drilling screws. Then install concrete and finish at the 10 inch gap. The best way is to completely install a new pool deck. This method is more expensive. However, your inground swimming pool will look brand new. The finish edge enhances and beautifies the pool's edge.

Your existing liner should be replaced after 10 years. After 8 years, the pattern should be faded and oxidized. When replacing a liner, use a white based pattern, a liner which will not show fading or discoloration due to pool chemical-oxidizing. The liner material is white on the backside, and has a printed pattern on the front. There are many styles to choose from.

There are some liners which are blue based and very attractive. These patterns will show discoloration and fading only after 2 years. However, special care can be taken to minimize fading and discoloration. You should use special alcohol based pool chemicals to maintain a nice looking pattern. These chemicals are more expensive and require more maintenance.

Liners are available in 20, 25, 30, and 40 mil thickness. 20 mil is sufficient and is a lot easier to work with. Also 20 mil liners easily expand/contract with extreme temperature changes. Whichever thickness you choose, the printed pattern will last the same amount of time. 30 and 40 mil liners can easily contract in the winter and pull from pool corners. You may find it impossible to reinstall the liner into the concrete finish edge. The 20–25 mil liner is easily reinstalled into the receiver even after contracting from the pool finish edge. If your pool liner is properly fitted, and installed few problems will occur, if any.

The key to proper liner installation is a perfectly fitted lining. Proper and extensive measurements should be taken and submitted to a swimming pool manufacturer. The first measurements are the pool size. For example, if your pool is 16 x 32 ft., it is probably not exactly 16 ft wide x 32 ft long and many pool manufacturers specifications are different. So measure exact points to ensure a proper fit. Measure width and length every 4 ft. and record square measurements.

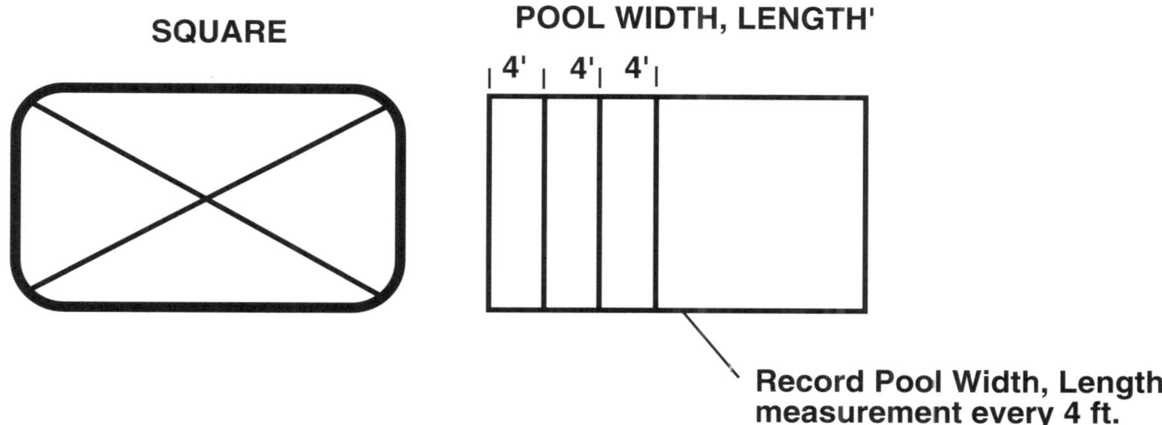

Next, record pool bottom measurements. Refer to the section on pool bottom design to identify shallow end, incline, etc.. Measure sidewalls and depth.

A perfectly fitted liner is an absolute necessity for enhancement and optimum pool function. There is no reason for an improperly fitted liner.

Your pool walls are steel, aluminum, or structural foam. Steel and aluminum walls are subjected to pool leaks and must be sanded, primed and painted. This is easily accomplished. Use zinc primer and special paint. Be sure to reseal joints with pure 100% silicone. Structural foam pools should require little or no preparation. However, foam may be fractured and require patching.

Next, your pool bottom must be prepared. The most common bottom is vermiculite/portland mixture. You should completely resurface the pool base before installing a new liner. Sand bottom pools should be replaced with vermiculite/portland. Sand bottoms are not a very good base, and deformations will occur frequently.

Sand-concrete bottoms are common and can be resurfaced with vermiculite/portland. Be sure to resurface your pool base. A smooth looking liner finish will look nicer and extend your pool life.

Skimmers, inlets, and maindrains can be replaced and installed. Saw cut your existing pool deck, and remove the old components. Install a brand new skimmer, inlet and main drain. You will extend the life of your pool and eliminate many repairs. Your inground pool will look brand new and be functionally sound.

Underground plumbing, discussed at the beginning of this section, can be easily replaced. Simply bypass the existing line and replace with a new plumbing line. Usually 100 psi poly pipe is used: heated, double clamped and glued. Although spa hose can be used, it is relatively expensive.

Your pool deck can be repaired, replaced or resurfaced with a rubber-like material. Resurfacing is common and rubber coating patterns are attractive and functional. The cost may be prohibitive to resurface your existing deck in addition to other alterations. Concrete resurfacers are sometimes considered by the budget-minded. The best method and most cost effective is to replace an existing deck with a new concrete or exposed aggregate pool deck. New concrete will enhance and help your inground swimming pool look brand new.

Rebuilding an inground pool completely will extend your pool life to compare with that of a new pool. Rebuilding costs are justified to provide decreased repairs, less maintenance and improved swimming pool appearance. Costs should be considered and amortized over the length of time a pool can be used. Rebuilding your inground pool is intelligent and cost efficient.

Finish & Expansion Joints DECKING

Pool Decking is a very important part of your new inground swimming pool. Decking must be planned, designed, and poured properly, and near perfect to ensure longevity and to enhance your pool area. There are several types of decking. We will discuss concrete:

Concrete is the most popular and widely used deck material. Concrete will last for years if properly installed. First you must excavate 8 inches below the proposed concrete deck elevation. Then fill in 4 inches of pea-gravel so any water will flow under concrete, eliminating water freezing and concrete fracture. Four inches of pea-gravel will prevent settling, ground shifting and earth movement.

Four inches thickness of concrete will provide plenty of support; however 5-6 inches will last longer. Four inches is standard, and will be sufficient. The only problem with concrete is the expansion that occurs in the winter months. It is best to install expansion joints every 5 ft. so the concrete will fracture at each joint. Concrete decking near the pool area is also subjected to pool splash water, rain, and intense sunlight. Be sure to seal your new concrete deck with a special clear sealer.

Expansion joints look very nice when troweled-in by hand. You can also cut-in joints with a concrete saw. Saw cuts must be near perfectly straight, and a good concrete man may have problems with straight cuts because of the landscaping around the pool. The best thing to do is have the joints troweled-in by hand and slightly cut-into joints the next day with a saw, then seal with sik-a-flex, an expandable concrete silicone. **Note;** be sure to install felt expansion joints where old concrete slabs join the new pool deck, and when a sidewalk or additional patio is poured.

Concrete must be properly leveled and finished. To perfectly level concrete when skreeting, take your time and have a experienced finisher present.

When finishing concrete do not spray water on the concrete surface. You will reduce the strength of the concrete on the surface and later chipping will occur.

A near perfect concrete deck is accomplished with minimal finishing time, and your pool area will look fine for years to come.

DECKING Wire Mesh Reinforcement

Wire mesh should be installed to help strengthen and prevent cracking. It is a thick metal, a fence-like roll; 5 x 150 ft, that is pulled-up into the wet concrete, as you pour.
Wire mesh must be bonded (grounded) to a copper ground rod, and inspected before you pour the concrete decking. Rebar can be installed to help support and strengthen your swimming pool deck. Rebar must also be bonded. You can use a Fiber-mesh concrete mix which will strengthen concrete and extend the life of the decking. Fiber-mesh consists of small plastic strands mixed into the concrete mix by the ready-mix companies. Fibers will show-up on the concrete surface; but later, they will wear-off.

Sona-tubes can be installed as additional support to your pool decking. 8 inch diameter tubes are positioned on top of the underground footing, connecting the pool decking to the concrete footing. The tubes are poured with concrete at the same time the deck is poured, and act as a pillar support system. You will have very few, if any fractures in your concrete decking for years if you install sona-tubes every four ft. at the pool perimeter. Sona-tube concrete support pillars decrease and eliminate concrete stress, eliminating fractures.

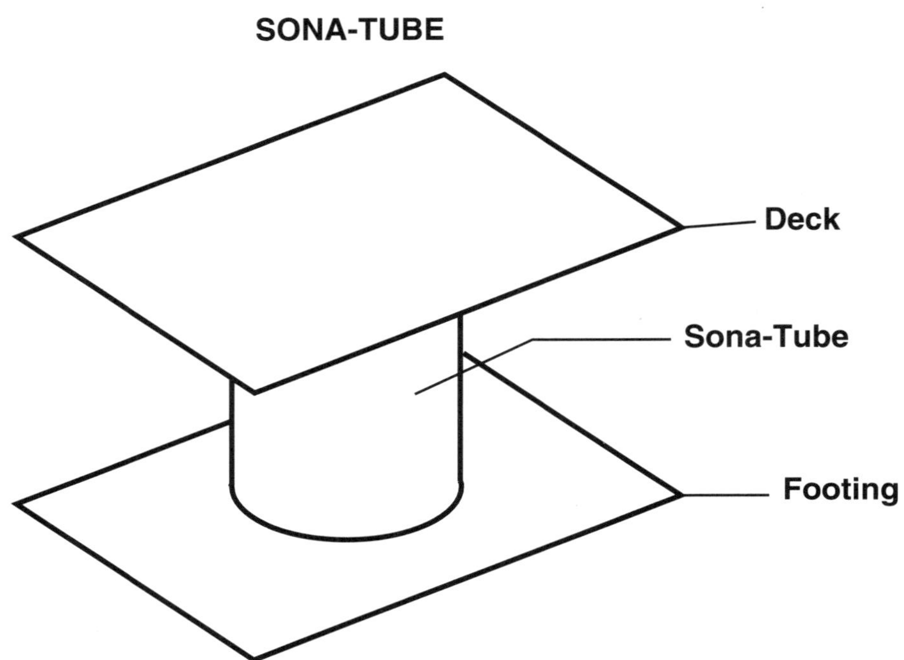

Skimmers/Div. Board Jig DECKING

Skimmers must be installed correctly relative to the pool decking. An extension ring must be placed over the skimmer body. The ring will greatly help in the adjustment of the skimmer top plate. The plate should be adjusted at the exact concrete grade height. To adjust, use duct tape and a piece of lumber. After the adjustment is made, remove skimmer top plate and tape.

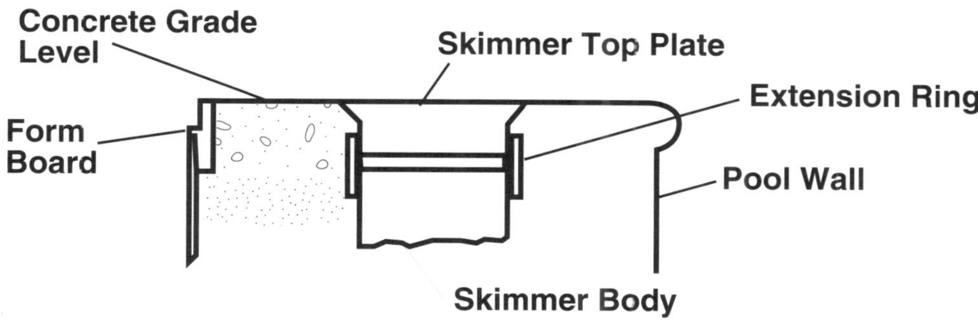

Diving board jigs must be positioned at the exact center of the deep end. Jigs are installed to the diving board manufacturer's specifications. The threads must be covered with cover provided and taped. Be sure enough threads are exposed so you can mount the diving board stand. Do not install diving board until the concrete decking is somewhat cured. (6-10 days).

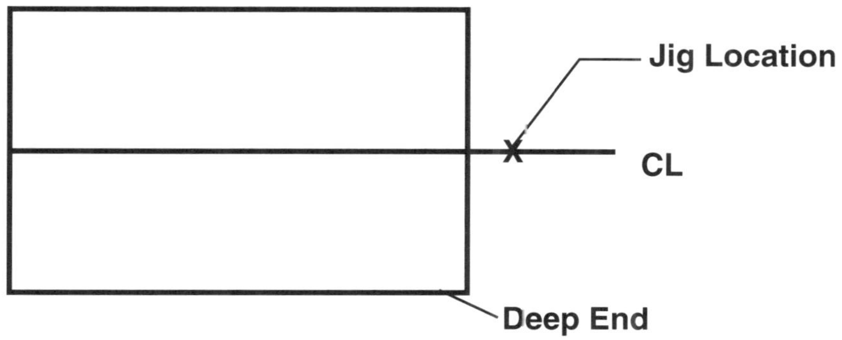

Ladders and handrails must be installed level, square and uniform to the pool shape. Use a piece of metal to support ladders/handrails and maintain an exact position that will not change during the concrete pour. The piece of metal must be a G-235 14 gauge steel so it will not rust.
You can attach it with a steel stake:

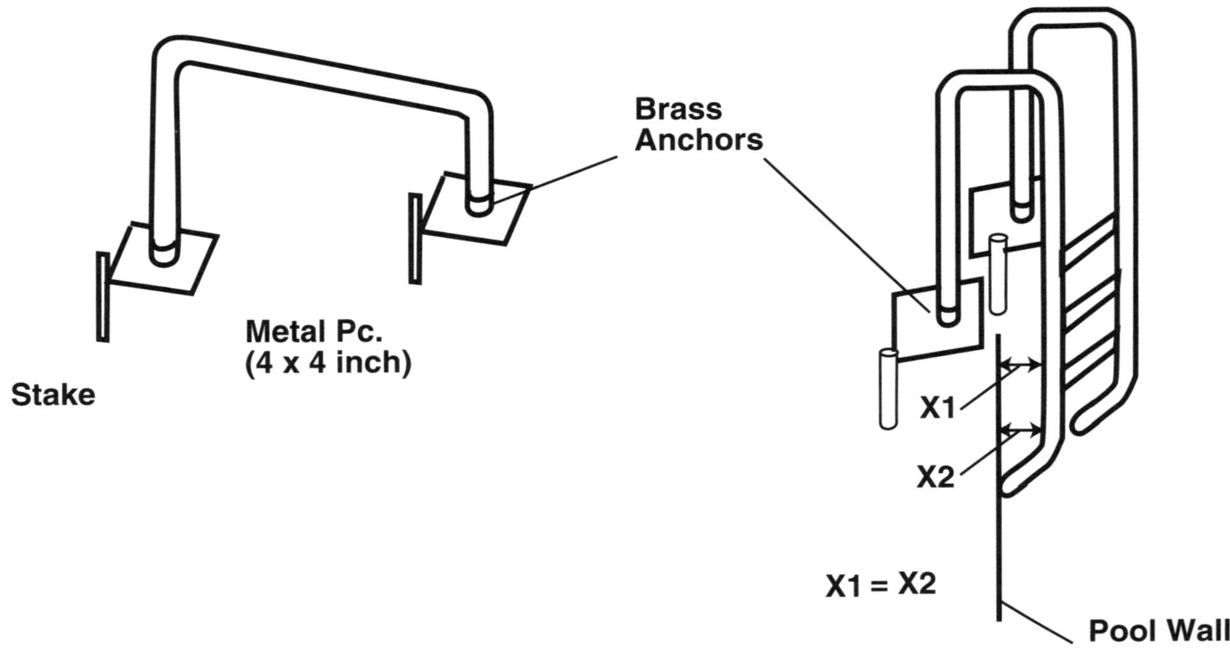

GENERAL OVERVIEW

When buying an inground swimming pool, first consider the best equipment: pumps, filters, heaters, etc.. Then consider a max-flo plumbing system that will adequately mix the water evenly with chemicals and heat. Pool function is extremely important so the best possible system should be implemented. Overrate pumps, filters, heaters and implant maintenance-free accessories like automatic chlorinators, 24 hour timers, automatic cleaners and poly mesh covers. If your budget doesn't allow them, then add them as you can. Solar reels and covers are becoming essential to improved pool care.

There are a great variety of pools to choose from. Most people will choose liner pools because of reduced cost and maintenance. Liner pools are installed in the northern climates and gunite/concrete in the south. A pool is a lot like a house. It is a land improvement which is permanently in place over a period of many years. Property taxes are slightly increased because of the increase in property value, around $100 a year. You should consider the cost of your pool over the time you will be living at a residence.

A pool pump draws at roughly 10-14 amps. Electric costs are usually $20.00 a month. Chemical costs are usually $100 a year. These questions are asked frequently and by following this guide you can reduce your cost substantially. If you cannot fit an inground pool into your budget, then consider a whirlpool.

Owning a whirlpool can help you to understand pumps, filters, chemicals, etc.. A whirlpool installed in your basement can be used year round. Inground pools are appreciated more in colder climates because of the winter down-time. Pools are used 6-7 months a year, which is plenty for most people. In fact, a winter break is refreshing and stimulates more interest.

Ponds are attractive and can become a focus and social area. A 20 X 25 ft. pond can greatly add beauty to a home. They are functional and practical. Waterfalls, fountains and lighting can contribute to the surrounding area. Fish, aquatic life and plants will stimulate the pond area creating an ecosystem that will allow you to enjoy the area.

GENERAL OVERVIEW

There are several swimming pool manufacturers located throughout the country. Many manufacture pools while others make pool components and accessories. The best way to decide is to use a reputable dealer. He usually handles many different pools and accessories. Pool equipment selection is important. Carefully consider each component. Pumps should be quiet, powerful, and have an adequate warranty. Check their performance charts. Filters are to be manufactured of the best material available. Thermoplastic should be used for pools subjected to adverse weather conditions. For winterizing information refer to the winterizing section.

There are many pool heater manufacturers. Warranties range from 2-5 years. Natural gas heaters are most popular and should be installed. Electronic ignition is a money saving feature and may be purchased as an added option. Electric heaters are seldom used because of the high operating cost. Spas, however, use electric heaters.

Pool vacuuming kits should be of the highest quality. Large clear weighted heads are best. You can actually watch the debris being vacuumed in. Poles should extend to more than 16 ft. and extension attachments should be made to last for at least 5 years. Vacuum hose is important . Choose a 5 yr.. warrantied hose. Choose the more expensive, overrated chemicals. Cheap chlorine and algaecide provide immediate solutions, but may cause you problems later. The real trick is to buy bulk chemicals that will last for two years. Cheap imitation chemicals will fade pool bottoms, unbalance water, and increase the difficulty of managing pool water. Floaters are not required and may cause you problems.

Pool filter sand should be purchased at a swimming pool dealer. Purchase the highest quality available. Cheaper silicone sand will dampen pool performance. Solar covers can be 8-12 mils. Eight mil covers are a lot easier to handle, but twelve mil last a bit longer. Solar covers should be covered when not in use to extend their life. The intense sun will deteriorate any solar cover. Solar covers are water cooled. Bubbles are always in the downward position. Solar covers trap ultraviolet rays and cause water to slightly warm. Solar reel systems are usually aluminum and included parts should be high quality plastic or metal.

A clean pool will function better and last a lot longer. Pools that are improperly cleaned and maintained may cause additional expense. Extending pool and equipment life is important and worth while.

Operating procedure is important and should be followed faithfully. Consider the 24 hour timer and run the pump minimally 5 hours per night.

Handrails, ladders and other equipment should be cleaned and polished. Proper water balance will maximize their life.

Swimming pools are fairly easy to care for. Refer to the section on maintenance tips for tricks on easy pool care. Vacuuming, brushing and skimming should be minimal and pool use frequent. Summer is a fun time of year and a pool can add enjoyment and pleasure throughout the season.

Constructing an inground pool can be an interesting adventure. Pool plans, specification sheets and construction methods are vital information needed for proper installation. You can expect your pool to operate at maximum performance at the lowest cost available. Construction must be completed accurately. Precise and correct methodology is explained throughout this guide and can be reviewed when needed. Pools take time to construct. Allowing 2-4 weeks for completion is normal. Keep in mind that the pool deck must also be poured and landscaping completed. You will have a better idea of what landscaping is required after the pool is completed.

Planning is especially important. Using a site plan is vital to attain the proper appearance. Use the design worksheets to plan the pool location and landscaping. You can plan and design ponds and whirlpools as well. Ponds are very attractive and easily constructed. (Refer to the pond section) A well landscaped pond contains bushes, trees, mulch, lights, fountains, fish, frogs,etc.. Proper construction methods are explained in full detail.

Local building and zoning approval is required for pools. You can contact them for whirlpools and ponds as well. Most areas are reasonable when it comes to their construction. The building of pools, ponds and spas actually add money into the local economy. Their construction can only help the community.

INTERESTING FACTS

Water pressure (weight) is important in understanding swimming pools. The specific weight=weight/volume, water= 62.4 1b./ft.^{3}, so for every 1 ft. of water, there is a weight of 62.4 1b./ft.^{3} thus a pool that is eight feet deep has a downward weight = 62.4 X 8= (500 lb. per 1 ft.^{2})

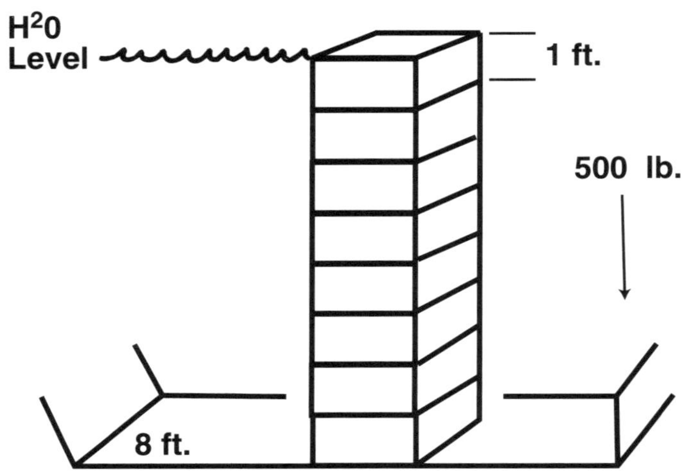

The water column shows 500 lb. of force on a square area=1 ft. or 1 ft. wide x 1 ft. length= 1 ft^2. The pressure on this area is 500 1b/ft.^{2} This can be converted to inches pressure - p=3.47 1b./in.^{2} or 3.47 psi. So the pressure is relatively small per square inch.

Pressure is greatest at the pool deep end. You can virtually calculate the weight of water in the pool. Simply calculate the square footage in the swimming pool: 16 X 32: (L X W X H). Volume $\triangleq$ (16 X 32 X 5) ft. $\triangleq$ 2560 ft. 2560 x 62.4 1b. $\triangleq$ 159,744 lbs. of water. That's a lot of water weight! However, pools are designed to withstand a great deal of water pressure. You can see that most pools only have bottom pressure=3.47 psi which is very small. The large weight is distributed to a large surface area.

PLANNING GUIDE

A handy guide and aid in planning. Simply establish a suitable scale and design your beautiful pool or pond and surrounding landscape enhancements accordingly.

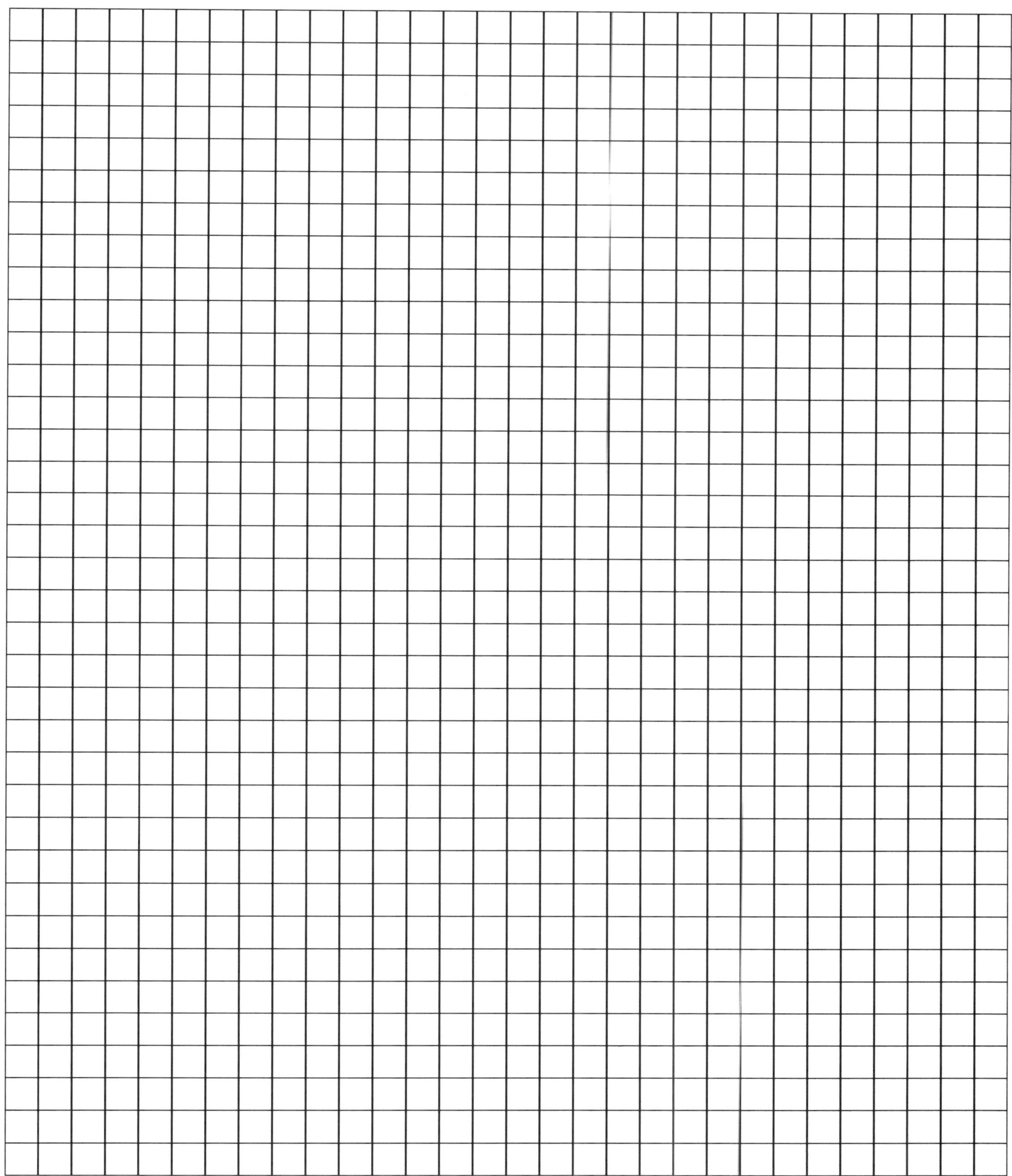

PLANNING GUIDE

A handy guide and aid in planning. Simply establish a suitable scale and design your beautiful pool or pond and surrounding landscape enhancements accordingly.

PLANNING GUIDE

A handy guide and aid in planning. Simply establish a suitable scale and design your beautiful pool or pond and surrounding landscape enhancements accordingly.

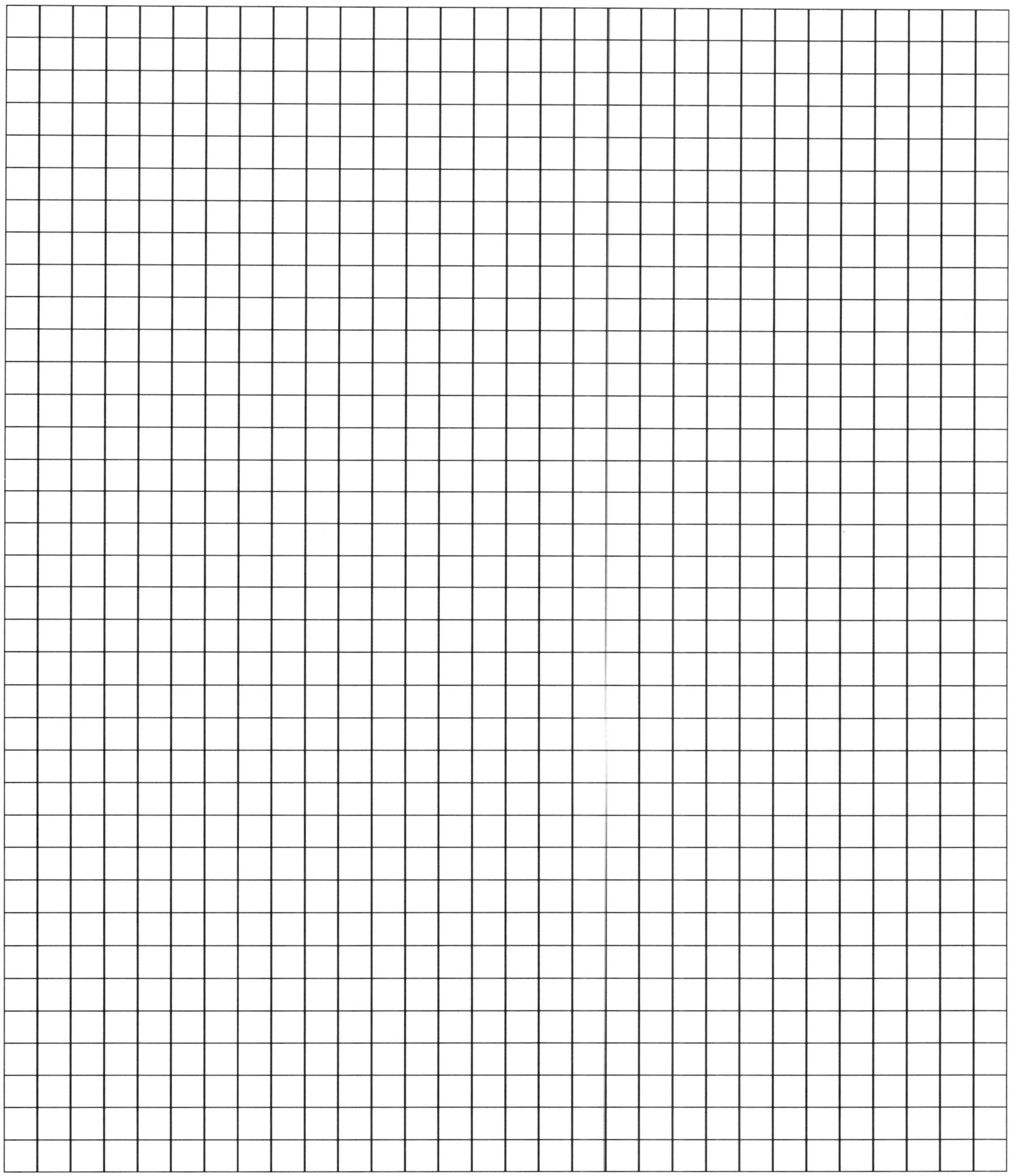

FOLIAGE ENHANCEMENTS

A handy guide to help you plan shrubbery and tree placement around your pool or pond. Simply clip, arrange and paste elements to design landscape enhancements suitable to your desires

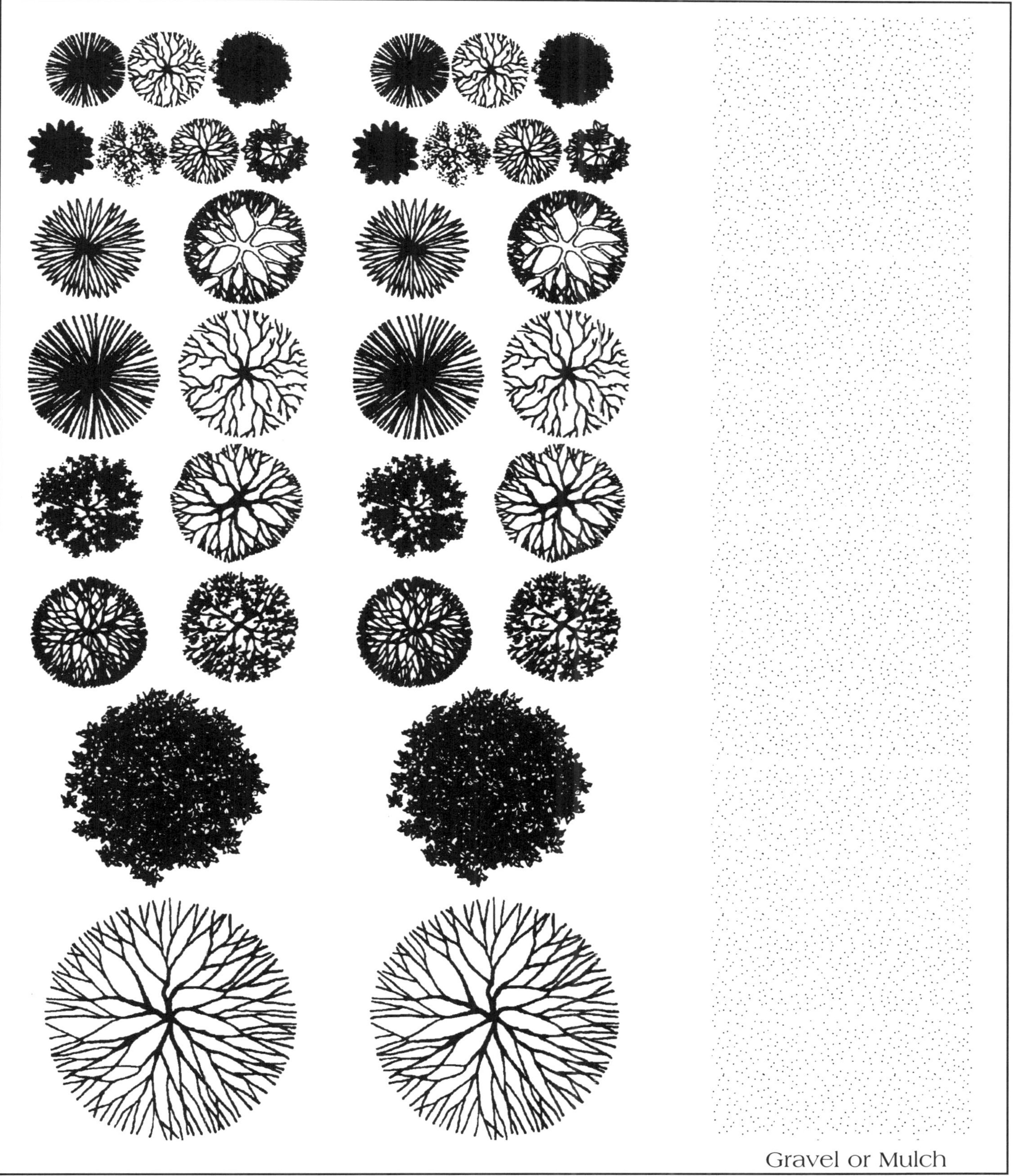

FOLIAGE ENHANCEMENTS

A handy guide to help you plan shrubbery and tree placement around your pool or pond. Simply clip, arrange and paste elements to design landscape enhancements suitable to your desires

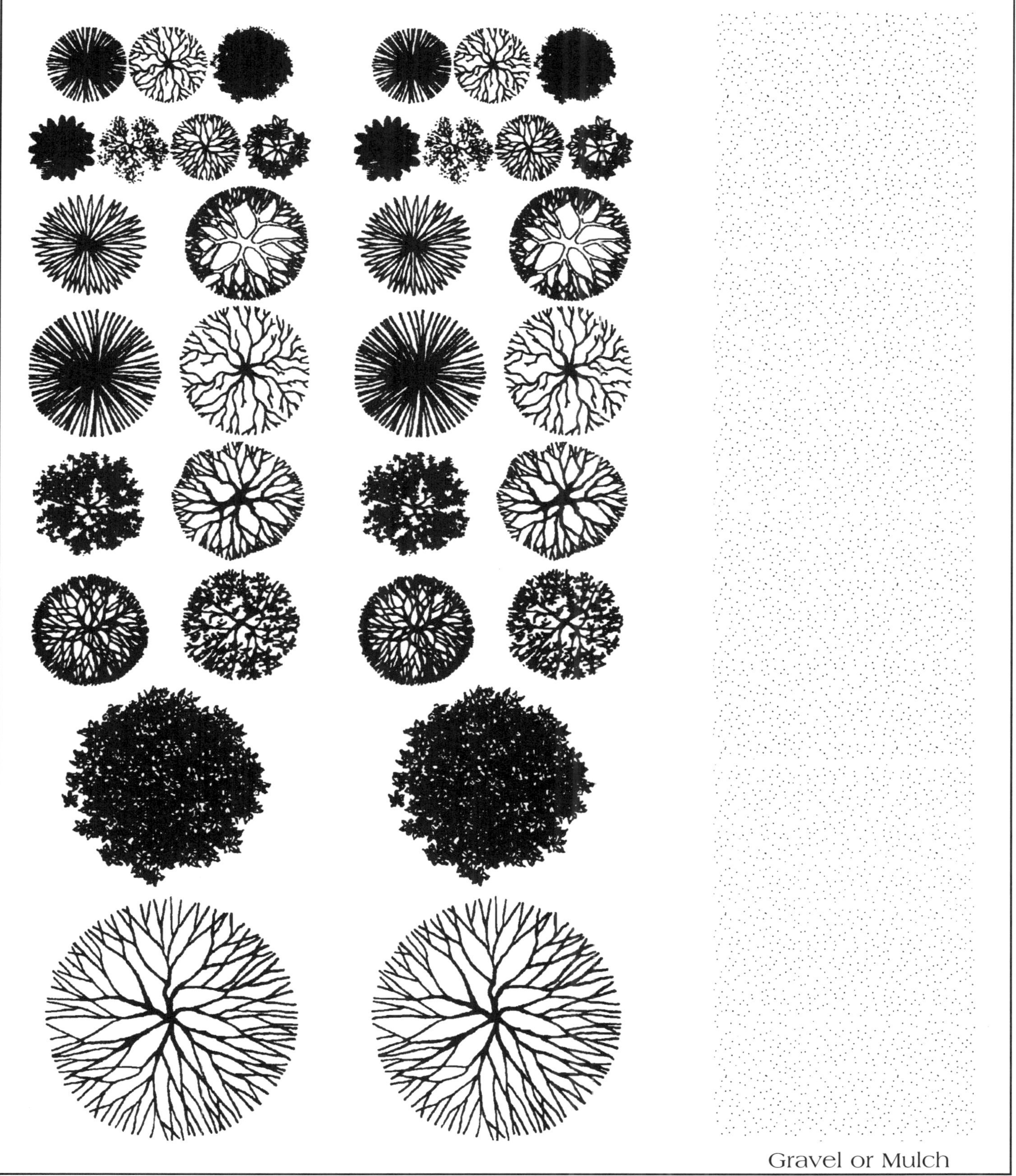

FOLIAGE ENHANCEMENTS

A handy guide to help you plan shrubbery and tree placement around your pool or pond. Simply clip, arrange and paste elements to design landscape enhancements suitable to your desires

Gravel or Mulch

CHEMICALS & MAINTENANCE TIPS

CHECK LIST

AUTOMATIC 24 HR. TIMER ___YES ___NO

OFF-LINE CHLORINATOR ___YES ___NO

AUTOMATIC CLEANER ___YES ___NO

SOLAR POOL/COVER ___YES ___NO

POOL CHEMICALS____

____

____

FILTER: SAND EARTH CARTRIDGE

PUMP (H.P.): .75 1.0 1.5

HEATER SIZE: 125,000 150,000 175,000 200,000 250,000 300,000

VACUUM KIT: ___YES ___NO

TYPE: ___CLEAR WEIGHTED ___NON WEIGHTED

BRUSH ___YES ___NO

NEW CONSTRUCTION WORKSHEET

Pool Shape:______________________________

Pool Size: ______________________________

Pool Type: ______________________________

Utilities: ______________________________

Electric/gas ______________________________

Phone ______________________________

Natural gas ______________________________

Diggers hotline (phone number): ______________________________

Septic system (yes) (no)

Location: ______________________________

Home water supply (well) (City)

Well Location:______________________________

Sump pump (outlet) (yes) (no)

Location: ______________________________

Foundation Tiles (yes) (no)

Location: ______________________________

Flood zone (yes) (no)

Cable T.V. (yes) (no)

Location: ______________________________

Proposed pool position ______________________________

Pool grade elevation ______________________________

Retaining Wall (yes) (no)

Location: ______________________________

Berms (yes) (no)

Location: ______________________________

Control Center

Position ______________________________

Additional information: ______________________________

____

NEW CONSTRUCTION

POOL

Pool Size: ______________________

Pool Style: ______________________

Pool Bottom: ______________________

Wall: ______________________

Deck Support System: ______________________

Finish edge at concrete: ______________________

FILTRATION SYSTEM: ______________________

Pump: ______________________

Pool Type: ______________________

Maintenance Kit: ______________________

Timer: ______________________

Auto Chlorinator: ______________________

Ladders: ______________________

Handrails: ______________________

Automatic cleaner: ______________________

Heater: ______________________

Diving Board: ______________________

Stairs: ______________________

Light: ______________________

Transformer: ______________________

Slide: ______________________

Solar Cover: ______________________

Chemicals: ______________________

Cover: ______________________

Other: ______________________

Other: ______________________

____

POND WORKSHEET

Pond ____

Pond Size: ____

Pool Shape: ____

Color: Black Blue White

Stone: Lanin Flag

Landscaping: Mulch Washstone

Bushes: ____

Trees: ____

Filtering system: ____

Lights: ____

Fountains: ____

Air bubbler: ____

Drain: ____

Waterfall: ____

Fish: ____

Aquatic life: ____

Plants: ____

WATER READINGS

To improve pool water conditions and solve water problems

	Chlorine	P.H.	Temp./cond.
EXAMPLE:	1.0 ppm	7.8	75°/sunny
Sunday	________	________	________
Monday	________	________	________
Tuesday	________	________	________
Wednesday	________	________	________
Thursday	________	________	________
Friday	________	________	________
Saturday	________	________	________

MAINTENANCE

(Planned method to improve pool care)

DATE:

__________ Sunday: ____

____

____

__________ Monday: ____

____

____

__________ Tuesday: ____

____

____

__________ Wednesday: ____

____

____

__________ Thursday: ____

____

____

__________ Friday: ____

____

____

__________ Saturday: ____

____

____

NEW CONSTRUCTION

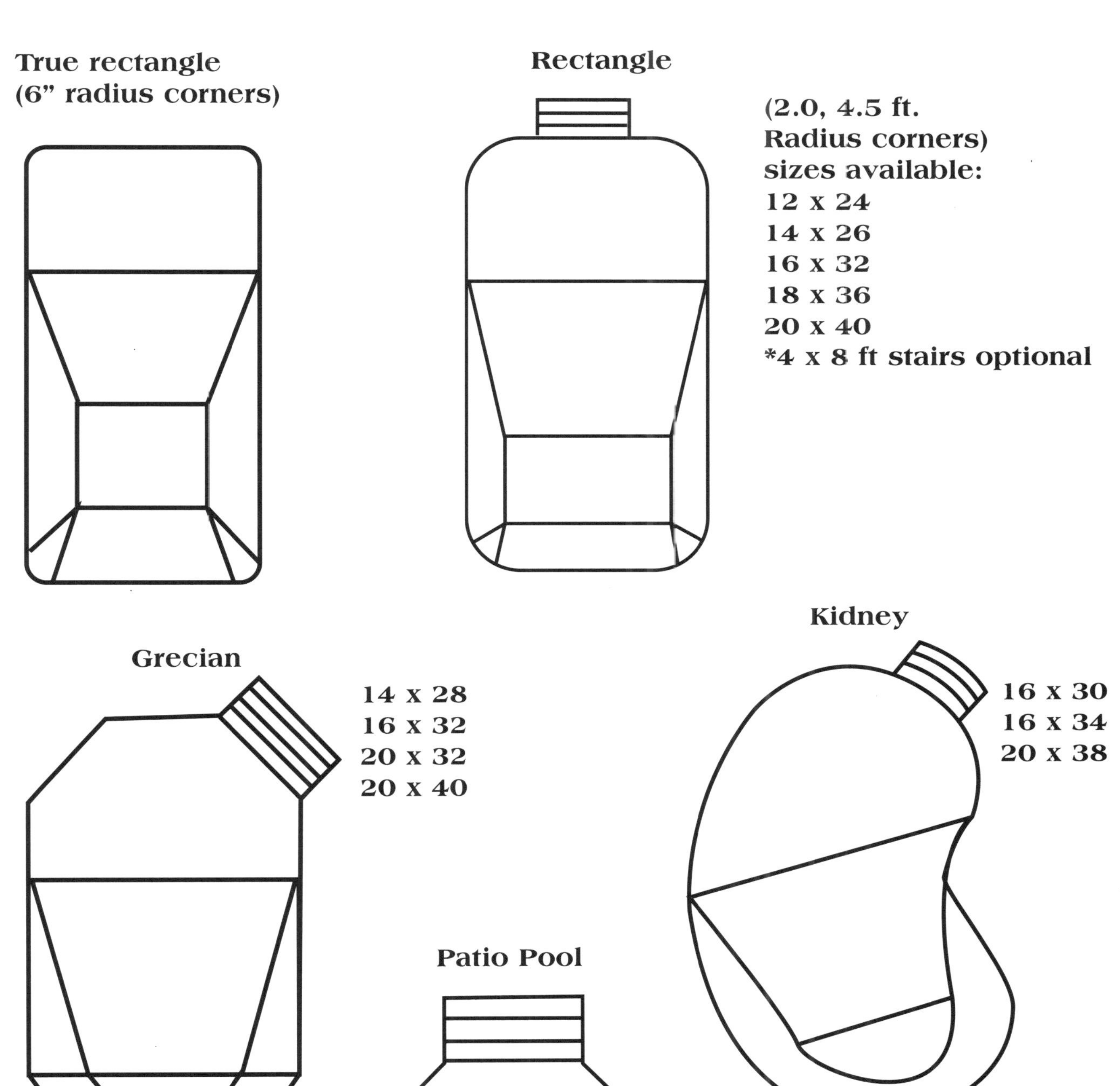